Michael Twaddle

Also by Lucy Mair

Primitive Government
New Nations
Witchcraft
Anthropology and Social Change
An Introduction to Social Anthropology
Marriage
African Societies
African Kingdoms

Anthropology and Development

Anthropology and Development

Lucy Mair

MACMILLAN PRESS
LONDON

First published 1984 by
THE MACMILLAN PRESS LTD
London and Basingstoke
Companies and representatives throughout the world

ISBN 0 333 36370 1 (hard cover)
ISBN 0 333 36371 X (paper cover)

Printed in Hong Kong

Contents

Acknowledgements

The author and publisher wish to thank the following who have kindly given permission for the use of copyright material: Penguin Books Ltd for an extract from Walter Elkan, *An Introduction to Development Economics* (Penguin Education, Revised edition 1976) p. 141. Copyright © Walter Elkan, 1973. Reprinted by permission of Penguin Books Ltd; and the Reserve Bank of India for the extract on pages 64–5.

1

What is Development?

What is Development?

In its basic meaning the word 'development' refers to a process, and in contemporary contexts the process is a movement towards a condition that some of the world's nations are supposed to have attained. Those which have not yet reached it used to be called 'underdeveloped'. This offended them, and now they are said to be 'less developed'; LDCs (less developed countries) is no longer a colloquial abbreviation but a technical term. The 'developed' ones may be called, quite simply, rich.

The rich nations are, for the most part, in the northern hemisphere; they are the ones that are called, with a fine disregard for geography, 'the West'. Those in the south who have earned the distinction of riches have been settled and dominated by migrants from the north. 'Development' involves, in one way or another, the relations between the rich nations and those for whom we sometimes prefer euphemisms for the word 'poor'.

The idea of development, if not the word, is as old as the expansion of Europe, and, interestingly enough, in all the interpretations that it has been given, there has been present some notion of duty. What has changed has been the answer to the question to whom the duty is owed.

In the earliest phase the duty is to God. It can be seen as an element in the conception of the calling, the task given to man to make more productive the world in which he has been set as God's steward. This is the message of the Parable of the Talents, of the steward who was condemned because he did not increase the value of the money entrusted to him. It followed that in lands which the inhabitants were failing to exploit to the full, in the original neutral meaning of that verb, others must do it for them.

This conception of man's duty to his maker was allied to the high value set on diligent work as something required of all men, and the importance of inculcating this value in populations to whom it was foreign. Such ideas are not in themselves ignoble; to say so is not to deny that they provided justification for many self-interested actions.

Another respectably old attitude to what is now called the allocation of resources is what Swift put into the mouth of the king of Brobdignag, that whoever could make two blades of grass grow where one grew before would deserve better of mankind than 'the whole race of politicians put together'.

Coming nearer to our own times and to the final period of British expansion (and to a use of the word not found in the *Shorter Oxford Dictionary*), we find that Joseph Chamberlain conceived his duty to lie in a different direction. His metaphors were more secular, though they doubtless derived ultimately from the same source. Britain had possessions, he remarked, which were almost unexplored and entirely undeveloped. 'What would a great landlord do', he asked, 'in a similar case with a great estate?' And in a phrase made famous as the epigraph to Lugard's *Dual Mandate in Tropical Africa* (1922) he said, We develop new territories as trustees for civilization, for the commerce of the world.' For him, then, it was to the other rich nations that those who possessed colonies owed a duty; he meant that we allowed traders and investors of other nations to operate freely in the territories that we controlled.

In the present century, the metaphor of trusteeship in relation to development came into vogue in another sense, as the reflection of its use in the Covenant of the League of Nations, in the article (22) that deals with what were called the Mandated Areas, the former German colonies which were left in the hands of the military forces of the Allies but not allowed to be annexed outright. Their populations were described – accurately at that date – as 'not yet able to stand by themselves', and their 'well-being and development' was stated to be a 'sacred trust of civilization'. The metaphor here is the relation between a trustee and a minor. The trustee must keep his ward's property intact, improve it if he can, but not divert it to his own use, and hand it over when the ward comes of age. But the principles held to be implied in a policy of trusteeship were confined to the prevention of abuses; development as an active policy was taken for granted and not examined. The wards were not to be deprived of land adequate for their needs, and they were not to be subjected to compulsory labour for private profit. For another decade and a half, in Britain at any rate, this was considered to be enough.

The next shift in attitude in Britain was brought about by serious rioting in the West Indies in the late 1930s, which was followed by the appointment of a Royal Commission to investigate the condition of the islands. Its report described them as 'a tropical slum'. Then for the first time Britain abandoned the principle that the colonies must be self-supporting, and decided to make sums available from the British Treasury for 'development and welfare'. As part of the preparation for reconstruction at the end of the Second World War, the colonies were invited to submit development proposals, and these turned out to be rather in the nature of letters to Santa Claus. The development section of the package consisted mainly of much-needed extensions of the infrastructure – feeder roads to cash-cropping areas, water supplies and the like. The sums to be allocated to development were spread very thin, but they slowly increased from year to year. The French government at the end of the war created a corresponding fund for the territories that were then called 'Overseas France'. Italy had made development grants to Ethiopia and Somalia during the brief period of Italian colonial rule.

Development in the Post-colonial World

As the colonial territories became independent, the conception of a duty towards the populations over which a European power exercised authority began to be merged in a wider feeling that the rich countries collectively had a responsibility towards the poor ones. So now the rich countries are no longer developing the poor ones, either their populations or their resources; the poor ones – now called 'less developed countries' or LDCs – are demanding development for themselves. Nor are the former colonial powers the leading investors in

development. During the years 1956–63 the total money
contributions to 'aid', as it is now called, nearly doubled, and
over half came from the United States. All the rich nations now
take part in what can almost be considered a fashionable
activity, and so do the various international organizations
concerned with economic matters, the United Nations, the
World Bank, the European Economic Commission, the
Organization for Economic Co-operation and Development.
   This is not a display of altruism on a global scale. Aid to
LDCs increases the exports of the rich countries, and specific
technical projects give employment to contractors; development itself, one might say, has become a growth industry. But it
is not a mere disguise for self-interest either; one element in the
political support for 'aid' policies is a genuine belief that the
rich countries should contribute what they can to the welfare of
their poorer neighbours.
   To some spokesmen of the LDCs, the goal of development is
essentially political – to reach what is called a 'mature
economy' of 'self-sustaining growth', that is one in which
increases in productivity are generated from within the structure and do not depend on outside assistance. In this vein Seers
(1969) writes of 'citizenship of a nation that is truly independent both economically and politically in the sense that
the views of other governments do not largely predetermine his
own government's decisions'. This condition would be more
readily conceived as an ideal by those with political responsibilities than by the citizens whom they govern.
   Measured quantitatively, development is an increase in gross
national product or in per capita income (taking the average of
the entire population embraced in a single fiscal system).
Growth rates are the only readily calculable measure, and a
slow growth rate is generally considered to indicate an
unhealthy economy. But a large body of opinion holds that a
high growth rate by itself leaves many problems unsolved.
Adherents of this view sometimes *define* development in a
manner that implies 'If it doesn't work out as I would like it, it
isn't development.' This is illogical, but it is perfectly reasonable for anyone to indicate what he thinks the aim of the
increase in growth should be. The following summary of these

aims would probably command widespread agreement: 'Improvement in the quality of life of all the people in a country . . . alleviation of poverty, ignorance and disease . . . to apply to everyone and not just a privileged élite, (Seers, 1969). The Government of India in introducing its five-year plan for 1969–74 observed that a higher growth rate and an increased equality in terms of consumption are mutually compatible objectives of planning and implementation are conceived along appropriate lines, and this might have been echoed by the governments of all the other LDCs. Whether the goal of equality is an illusory one is a question to be discussed in its place (Chapter 6). The conception of a 'poverty line' below which, in an ideal world, nobody would be allowed to fall, is more modest, provided a satisfactory definition of unacceptable poverty can be found.

By the standards of the World Bank, 40 per cent of the world's population – some 800 million people – are living in conditions of poverty and semi-starvation; nine-tenths of these are farmers or rural wage-labourers. The Bank now advocates a strategy that is not content with measuring increases in total national product. A report which it published in 1978, and which was announced as the first of an annual series on world development, remarked that 'the poor are apt to be bypassed by growth', and concluded that 'modifications in the pattern of growth to increase the productivity of the poor must be central to an effective attack on poverty'. This had has the result that agriculture has received much more attention than it had before, but not that particular attention has been given to the very poorest farmers. Many agrarian policies are criticised on this ground, an attitude which stems from Lenin's hostility to the Kulaks or better-off Russian peasants.

Michael Lipton (1974) criticises a view which is common to most of the governments that claim to be socialist: that development consists, and must consist, in industrialization, and that the peasant's role is to produce a surplus of food to supply the workers in industry. This has been imposed in communist countries – notably the USSR – by forced deliveries of foodstuffs. Elsewhere government policies have aimed at keeping down the price of food, and revolutionary activists urge peasants to accept low prices for the sake of their comrades in the cities. As Lipton points out, economic policy is made in cities where bureaucrats and legislators are gathered, and where the resentment of wage-earners at a rise in the cost of food is quickly felt (and in India, the country he has chiefly in mind, their wages are low enough in all conscience). Employers and workers are, then, at one in wishing to keep down the price of food. In addition the price of fertilisers is unnecessarily high because of the protection given to local producers. Well-to-do farmers can buy fertilisers and other costly inputs, and so can sell their produce in bulk in urban markets, even at artificially low prices. But the poorer peasant who grows only enough to live on, with perhaps a small surplus to meet cash needs, remains as poor as before. Lipton adocates the deliberate diversion of investment from industry and large-scale agriculture to works that can raise the productivity of the small farmer, the reduction of taxation in the rural areas, and more welfare provision in the country, particularly in the allocation of doctors and of devoted and properly trained extension workers. This view is gaining support; to some it points the way to a solution of the problem of rural poverty. But it is an economist's solution; it is about incomes, not people. Better prices encourage higher productivity certainly. But the re-organization of a labour force, or even of a labour day, is a matter of social, not economic, gains or losses.

A minority of voices recommend policies which concentrate entirely on small improvements in farming with small local industries. E. F. Schumacher's *Small is Beautiful* (1973) makes an eloquent plea for such a strategy, and an Appropriate Technology Group exists to put the case for it. Large-scale planners argue convincingly that the need to raise productivity in the LDCs is far too urgent to be met by such tiny improvements, and that by themselves they could never meet the demands that are being made for a rapid advance to self-sustaining growth; indeed some in the LDCs suspect that the current emphasis on 'helping the poorest' is nothing but a red herring, or a means of preventing them from competing with the industrialized countries. Many serious economists, however, are concerned that mechanization is reducing opportunities of employment in the rural areas while industrialization is not creating enough in the cities (Barker, 1978).

At what most people call 'grass roots' and one original writer (Minogue, 1980) 'platoon' level, one may look at different technical devices and see how far they come up to expectations in practice. Long ago the more observant agricultural officers in Nigeria set themselves to explode the assumption that what the farmers needed was a 'modern' plough which would not merely 'scratch the surface' but turn over the soil to the same depth as in Europe; they pointed out that the lighter African soils could not stand that kind of treatment. The Australian anthropologist and explorer Donald Thomson contrasted his experiences with camel and motorised transport; camels need water but trucks need petrol, and they are more flexible than trucks in other ways. In the same way, some observers have perceived practical disadvantages in tractors. Tractor-drawn ploughs are liable to break on rocks and stumps, so that if they are to be useful the ground must be cleared before ploughing starts. They must inevitably deteriorate in time, and the faster the more roughly they are handled. They need maintenance, and there may not be enough qualified mechanics available. In other words the tractor, if it is to do what is expected of it, must be part of a package which includes not only the training of drivers and mechanics and the import of spare parts in sufficient quantity, but also a reorganisation of other aspects of farming practice. A World Bank mission to Africa concluded that in many areas – and particularly where individual hold-ings are small – African farmers would do better to adopt ox-drawn ploughs (a solution which would itself imply the necessary changes in cattle management). On the other hand, there are regions where ox traction is not practicable because of the tsetse fly; and others where tractors have been introduced successfully (De Wilde, 1967). What matters is to avoid choosing *either* the modern just because it is modern *or* the simple just because it is simple.

One contributor to a symposium on these questions urged the development of a locally based institutional system which 'generates applied technology and effectively communicates it to cultivators' (Heady, 1978). This statement puts in general terms just what an anthropologist would try to recommend in the context of particular projects.

Development Policies

Policies intended to raise the productivity of agriculture, and thus the standard of living of the rural poor, consist in spreading knowledge of more efficient techniques and providing resources to enable farmers to adopt them. Enough land is, of course, the basic resource, and land reform – the redistribution of land – has been an important aspect of policy in many LDCs. Irrigation enables more land to be cultivated; it may make it possible to harvest two crops in one year. Credit is usually offered on easy terms for the purchase of fertilisers, pesticides or whatever the farmer is being advised to use. Particular areas – usually irrigated – may be offered for settlement on condition that the settlers follow prescribed cultivation patterns. Very often settlers are not interested in the first place, or leave the settlement after a short time. The reason is sometimes apparent to outsiders who have a close knowledge of the people concerned, and such persons are often, though by no means always, anthropologists.

Extension services for the dissemination of technical knowledge can be found in any country. In the LDCs they form part of plans for substantial investment in rural development projects. India has the most elaborate organization, set up with the first five-year plan in 1952. The aim of this policy was community development, that is the simultaneous and co-ordinated development of all aspects of community life. For this purpose the whole of India was divided into Community Development Blocks, each with a population of 60 – 100,000, and within each block ten Village Level Workers were responsible for direct contact with the rural population. From 1960 they were expected to devote four-fifths of their time to the promotion of improvements in agriculture; in particular they were expected to co-operate with the elected village councils which were set up at the same time. These are the people who need to know what the probable impact would be on the villagers of policies devised by higher authority. The criticism has been made that they are too often expected to put across a uniform 'package' of information, provided by experts with no direct knowledge of the populations to which they are to be offered (Hunter, 1970, p. 69).

India's five-year plans have been introduced with commitment to high ideals. The first declared as its aim the 'creation of conditions in which living standards are reasonably high, all citizens – men and women – have full and equal opportunities for growth and justice'. When agriculture was given priority, policy was to identify areas of 'quick response' and concentrate activity on them in an Intensive Agricultural Development Project recommended by the Ford Foundation. In 1965 came the High Yielding Varieties Programme which produced the 'green revolution'. 'Areas of quick response' must inevitably be those better endowed by nature, where some farmers are already prosperous, and by the time of the Fourth Plan it began to be felt unsatisfactory that there had been so little alleviation in the condition of the really poor. Special programmes were then introduced for small farmers and agricultural labourers and for drought-prone areas; the assistance given consisted in subsidising irrigation and credit on easy terms. Finally, a scheme for the development of desert areas was introduced in 1977–8. The latest five-year plan, for 1978–83, allocated 43 per cent of the total resources invested to rural development and agriculture; and the Government of India undertook to abolish unemployment and poverty within ten years (Azad, 1978). Brave words, indeed.

A mission from the World Bank to Tanganyika (as it then was) in 1961 contrasted two types of development, 'improvement' and 'transformation'. The first concentrates on the adoption of more efficient techniques within an existing social and economic structure. The second aims at transforming this structure. This itself may be pursued in two ways. One is the re-settlement of farmers and their families on holdings which they are expected, as a condition of their occupation, to cultivate by approved methods. Re-settlement may be accompanied by attempts to introduce new standards of housing and to extend education and other social services, as in the Volta Re-settlement Scheme which was carried out in Ghana. When that country created the largest man-made lake (at that time) in the world, it sought to provide improved standards in every aspect of life for the people who had to be moved from their homes (there are, of course, countries where this kind of change would not count as transformation). A more radical transformation –

if it can be successfully accomplished – is the creation of new institutions for decision making, as in the Ujama' a villages in Tanzania. A different method of transformation is to change the laws of land ownership, dispossessing large landowners and distributing their land among small holders. There have been land reforms in most of the LDCs; not all have been equally successful. Of transformation in that wider sense which aims at the creation of 'socialist man' this book will have a little, but not much, to say. The nations which have attempted it have associated it with the collectivisation of land.

What has the Anthropologist to say?

All development projects call for technical knowledge from a dozen different sources. Soil scientists know the best soils for different crops, agronomists the best way to cultivate them. There are water specialists who can calculate how many inches of water an irrigation system must supply to ensure that the crop gets enough. Engineers know how much water a dam must impound – and so how much land must be flooded – to supply a given amount of light and power, and how wide and deep a canal must be if it is to be used by a given type of shipping. Economists have ever more sophisticated techniques for calculating the probable results of the investment of resources in different sectors of a country's economy or in specific projects.

Anthropologists do not know this kind of thing, as they do not know the answers to the arguments bandied between economists about the overall consequences of different strategies of national investment. They have nothing to offer at that level, and it would be irrelevant and impertinent to ask economists operating at that level to listen to them. Their knowledge, like that of the other specialists just mentioned, can be brought to bear on *particular projects*, and especially rural projects, which affect the lives of identifiable populations, or may be expected to do so in a project which is under discussion. They rely on their general understanding of small-scale rural societies, supplemented here and there by observations of actual cases, on the basis of which it might be possible to do better next time. They can more often offer warnings than advice. But in addition to specific warnings, they can give to people responsible for the implementation of development projects, and possibly to outsiders called in to evaluate such projects, some indication of the essential information on the nature of the societies they are dealing with which may help them in the conclusions that they draw.

The strength of the anthropologist's approach, as Long (1977) has pointed out, is that it is 'actor-oriented'. It views the operation of development policies not from above, through the eyes of the policy-makers, but from below, through those of the supposed beneficiaries (not entirely in jest, some of us call them 'victims'). What is happening to them is a change in their environment; new demands may or may not be made on them by a superior authority, but in any case new opportunities are offered. The people who are being planned for are not an inert mass being worked upon and proving more or less recalcitrant. They are individuals perceiving the new environment as welcome or unwelcome – according to the values they have grown up with and each one's personal circumstances – and dealing with it, perhaps by rejection, but just as often by attempts to exploit it to advantage; such attempts, however, need not be what the policy-makers hope for. Different people will perceive different advantages and disadvantages, not only from the point of view of different value systems but from individual points of view within the same one. Pre-existing institutions and norms of conduct are not always obstacles to development; sometimes they are referred to in order to justify new strategies, and then they change without the actors being aware of it.

Only rarely and recently have anthropologists been invited to contribute to projects for development, and when they are invited they are seldom allowed the time that they would consider necessary to enable them to speak with real authority. Indeed one cost-benefit analysis has calculated that the advantage of the anthropologist's contribution is not worth the delay to the project that it entails. Recently an anthropologist employed by the Indonesian government was first offered two months and then had this cut down to one. But as he was the only member of the project team able to speak the local language, this was at least better than nothing. In the event he made a considerable number of pertinent suggestions, among them that irrigation facilities, which have often needed such complicated control that villagers could not work them, should be so devised that they could be managed by a small neighbourhood.

Most of our warnings are the fruit of studies made after the event, showing where some project has failed of its purpose because the circumstances have been misunderstood. This kind of warning, of course, has no effect unless later development workers read it, but one may mention at any rate one context in which they have done so. This is the re-settlement of large populations, particularly where the construction of dams has caused their homes to be flooded. The first detailed study of such a project – sponsored by research institutions, not by a development authority – was made by Colson (1971) and Scudder (1962) who traced in detail the story of four Gwembe villages in the south of Zambia which were moved on account of the building of the Kariba Dam on the Zambezi. They began by making a record of Gwembe social organisation and ecology, then visited the new homes shortly after the move, when it was still clearly recollected – by some people as a total disaster – and have made further studies to see how far the Gwembe have succeeded in coming to terms with their new environment. This unique long-term study has established Thayer Scudder as an authority on re-settlement schemes, particularly in connection with the man-made lakes which are being created in one LDC after another. The problems that such schemes create are important enough to deserve a chapter to themselves; they will be discussed in Chapter 8.

The stereotyped assumption in voluntary as well as enforced re-settlement schemes is that the ideal farming unit is the northern European and American 'homesteading' unit of a couple with their children; and further, that it is the man and his sons who actually work in the fields. This man is envisaged as an intelligent and ambitious fellow who will work hard with new crops and new methods for the sake of a better income.Too often in reality it is the woman who does the harder work and the man who gets the better income, and this is one reason why settlers on such schemes do not stay. Even anthropologists are only now beginning to turn their attention to the share of women in production, or their contribution to production by the maintenance of the home. In Rhodesia there has been for many years an arrangement whereby Africans of approved farming ability could buy land in certain limited areas. Only one complete family (man with wife or wives and unmarried children) could live on one holding. The houses were far apart, as they are in settlement schemes in Papua New Guinea; the reason in the latter case is said to be 'that the individual on his own land is an Australian ideal', and some such argument may have influenced the Rhodesians. In both cases the result was to cut people off from the neighbours with whom they were accustomed to co-operate in tasks calling for more labour than one household could provide. In Rhodesia the result was – again! – that women had to work harder, and they encouraged their daughters to marry boys from the 'undeveloped' areas held on traditional tenure, where life was easier even if incomes were lower.

Anthropologists in general have the reputation of always seeking to preserve what is traditional. If they do take that line, it is because the general thrust of development policies has always been in the direction of what an expert on fisheries once called 'bulldozing the tropics into civilisation'. Projects are devised by experts, whether national or foreign, who are themselves 'modern' or 'modernised', and who rarely have that close knowledge of rural conditions that would enable them to judge when and why institutions that they regard as anachronistic still serve a useful purpose. It is because this is the kind of situation most likely to be overlooked that anthropologists have emphasised it, and they do not assert that what is true of one population must be true of another. They only beg the agents of development to keep their eyes open.

We do not claim to have all the answers; we know how intractable the problem of poverty is, but the school of thought to which I belong does not believe there is any once-for-all way to solve it. To Marxists this is evidence of our false consciousness, or worse, our bad faith. We have to please, it is said, the governments who allow us to work in their countries, still more those who actually employ us as advisers, and certainly we would rather see plans for development succeed than not. We do not regard them as palliatives which enable exploiting rulers to maintain their hold, and thus postpone the day when the condition of the poor becomes so intolerable that the masses rise in revolt (and even then, a small voice says, there will be questions of the allocation of resources). I would myself agree with the writer, a socialist and a student of development planning, who repudiates 'the group that gleefully watches things getting worse in the belief that only then will they get better' (De Kadt, 1974, p. 12).

In the chapters that follow, then, I shall suggest what kinds of anthropological data can help those who are trying to make things better to avoid making them worse.

2

Modes of Livelihood

Among that quarter of the world's population living in the LDCs who are reckoned to be below the poverty line, the majority derive their subsistence – food and shelter – directly from the resources of their own environment. They live on grain that they grow themselves, or on the meat and milk of their herds, and build their own houses of local materials. Such peoples from time immemorial have bartered what surplus they had with their neighbours, and as trade relations have been extended they have come to produce a surplus for sale, and often to cultivate other crops in addition to those on which they depend for food. The majority have long been settled farmers, but a minority are still nomads whose basic resource is the herds of cattle, sheep, goats or camels with which they move regularly in search of grazing. There are also still a few populations which neither till the soil nor domesticate animals but live entirely on wild products, hunter-gatherers as they are called.

Nomadic Peoples

Development for nomadic peoples is commonly taken to mean first and foremost requiring them to settle in permanent homes, with the corollary that they must learn to farm. Cases can readily be quoted of misguided settlement policies which have had disastrous consequences. The history of the Indian reservations in the United States is the oldest, but it is now too far in the past to be relevant to the problems of development today.

For forest dwellers, development has sometimes meant the exploitation of their resources by outsiders, as has happened recently in the interior of Brazil, where roads were driven into

15

the forests and brought in mineral prospectors, as well as landless peasants from other parts of the country, themselves among the poorest Brazilians. But sometimes, as in the case of the Hadza of Tanzania, it has been thought good for the food gatherers themselves to give up their wandering way of life, settle down and learn to cultivate. The Hadza have not benefited much from this. In their former small, constantly moving bands, they did not need to know the principles of sanitation that are necessary for numbers of people concentrated permanently in one place, and they were soon devastated by fly-borne disease.

Pastoralists either move continually with their flocks (nomads) or drive them from wet to dry season pastures with the seasons (transhumants). Both types have a recognised homeland and recognised travel routes. Transhumants have a more circumscribed home, in villages within reach of permanent ground water for cooking and washing where, usually, the women and children stay when the men move away with their flocks; here some grain is grown.

A form of settlement that must have been going on all through a great part of history results from the free decision of nomads (the word can be allowed to stand for both types) to move to adequately watered lands, and either abandon cattle raising or combine it with more productive agriculture than could be practised in their earlier homes. In the conditions of today there may be more inducements for such a change than there were in the past. One very obvious one is the provision of permanent water by the sinking of boreholes, which forms a part of development plans in most countries with precarious rainfall. Another may be some opportunity to grow cash crops which is more profitable than selling milk, butter and hides. The most recent of all is that provision of welfare services which is now a commitment of all governments. In such spontaneous settlement each family, or a larger kin-group, decides where it will go; naturally the first to settle attract others from the same area. Most nomads love their flocks, but it is a mistake to suppose that they love them beyond all reason. Those who seek to solve development problems by the settlement of nomads need to know what makes them *want* to settle.

There may be different reasons in different cases. A study

recently made in Sudan (Holt and Abdalla, 1981) concerns sections of two different nomadic tribes who are becoming settled for different reasons and with different consequences. The populations concerned are called Zaghawa and Messiriya (Humr). The Zaghawa homeland is in the north of Darfur, the westernmost province of Sudan. They are traditionally trans-humant, growing millet wherever this is possible. A small number have been moving away to the south for a long time, as the pastures became overcrowded and their poor soils were exhausted, but the trickle became a flood during the disastrous drought of 1969–73. At this time they are believed to have lost four-fifths of their herds, largely by starvation, but also because they had to sell cattle to meet the cost of their journey.

Influential Zaghawa were divided in their attitude to piecemeal migration. One section opposed any move; the other favoured plans for a concerted move by a large number, and chose an area in the south where there was land available. The migrants themselves did not want to go so far, and most of them stopped much further north, near the provincial capital, El Fasher. Some of the tribe had gone there a long time before, although the area is badly off for surface water, the reason why there was empty land there. They have given up any idea of rebuilding their herds, though some may own cattle which are kept for them by kinsmen in the north. They are now cultivating larger areas than they could in their original homeland, but they tend to put what money they make into trade. Some of the settlements near El Fasher comprise over 1,500 people; in a region where 5,000 constitute a town, this gives them a strong claim on government for such welfare services as schools and clinics.

The Humr, whose home is on the border between Kordofan and the Bahr el Ghazal, are neighbours of the Dinka, whom anthropologists have correctly portrayed as the principal victims of Nuer cattle raids. But Dinka too can raid cattle, and Humr have been finding them uncomfortable neighbours, so much so that they abandoned a cash-cropping venture which they had started; in 1981, however, they made a peace agreement with the Dinka which seems to promise them a more secure life. What has attracted them to settle in numbers is the provision of bore-holes in southern Kordofan, which began in 1968.

In Dailim, one of the Humr settlements studied by these two authors, Humr and other neighbouring peoples have been gathering from the beginning of the century in numbers sufficient to build seven mosques and Koran schools. It seems to be a fallacy, then, to suppose that nomads will only settle if some catastrophe deprives them of their flocks. However, it is true that settling down does not by itself make them lose interest in cattle. Those Humr who have settled appear to own as many cattle as before, and still send them each year to dry-season grazing with one member of the family in charge. What they value, like the Zaghawa, is the availability of welfare services; but it is not certain that this is an attraction for all Humr.

Although Sudan is no less committed to planned develop-ment than other LDCs, this migratory process has not so far been brought under official control. By nationalising land the government has taken to itself the right to say who shall settle where, and as the source of welfare services it can always say who should have them. Unplanned migration in the southern Sudan may be a residue of the rebellious period when the writ of Khartoum did not run there. But, as the authors observe, the authorities 'tend to respond to the greatest pressure rather than to follow area-wide plans'. After all, this is one form of democracy.

In addition to its merit as a study which does not pose problems in terms of simple alternatives, this one places the alternatives for the nomads or ex-nomads in the context of the wider developments that affect their circumstances and so no doubt their choices. One change that is rarely taken into account when improvements in farming are described is the demand for the labour of young men and the improvements in communication which make it possible to engage in work a long way from home.

An alternative possibility for children who would in the past have been employed in herding is attendance at school – and one motive for settlement, as has been mentioned, is access to schools. Schooling in itself tends to make the younger gener-ation interested in other means of livelihood. It follows that in many contexts hired labour will be needed to replace family labour, and from this it further follows that the risks of loss in bad years are more serious. Holt and Abdalla predict that this will lead to the investment of more resources in cultivating and trading than in livestock.

It was no part of their brief to consider how to maintain the supply of meat and dairy products in these circumstances, and it would be for an economist to estimate the importance of the contribution of the nomads to it. The conventional wisdom of today looks to ranching in controlled grazing areas as the answer, and schemes of this kind were launched after the drought of 1969–73 in the Sahel, the area on the southern fringe of the Sahara in which the average annual rainfall is between 4 and 20 inches. The six states through whose territory the Sahel belt runs were all formerly French colonies, and the policies now favoured for its development are those advocated by the French during the colonial period, now intensified by the massive investment characteristic of United Nations projects. The plan adopted in Mali has been subjected to critical review by a journalist, Patrick Marnham (1979) and an anthropologist, Jeremy Swift (1978). It aims at the division of the region into areas for cereal farming with irrigation and for the intensive breeding of cattle and sheep. From these activities the inhabitants are expected to derive cash incomes to buy their food and other necessities, and so to be no longer at the mercy of their climate. And the effect will be to 'roll back the desert'.

The Tuareg (the nomadic population of northern Mali) have not been consulted about the future which is being prepared for them (assuming that plans which have been adopted are effectively implemented). Lords of the desert as they have been within living memory, they despise the settled life. As for their allegedly 'intolerable sufferings', they have evolved an adaptation to the extremes of climate without which they could hardly have survived through all these centuries. They rely on their herds mainly for milk, not meat; in the season when milk is short they buy or barter millet from the cultivators, selling their stock, or salt which they bring from the Saharan mines. It is camels and goats, not sheep and cattle, that produce milk through the greater part of the year.

Rainfall in the Sahel is quite unpredictable; there is no

recognisable cycle of drought and flood, the latter as serious a problem, and just as unpredictable. For the Tuareg, therefore, the first priority is to build up herd numbers to meet the risk of losses from either. At times when the animals are most numerous they lend some to the cultivators, and reclaim them when the numbers are depleted. It is not surprising that when they are offered the latest means of preventing stock diseases they accept them eagerly, and yet reject arrangements for the 'fattening of stock for slaughter-houses' (Marnham, 1979, p. 10). This is what has caused the overstocking that is now ruining the pastures.

Overgrazing is deplored (rightly) because it destroys the vegetation that retains the top soil. Goats are always held to be particularly destructive because they browse on the bark of trees. But what of *people* who cut down trees for firewood? The effect of 'development', even on the small scale that has been attained so far, has been that more trees are cut down for fuel than many hundreds of goats could have killed. People in Ouagadougou (the capital of Upper Volta, just south of the Sahelian region) have to spend 25 per cent of their income on firewood because there is none within forty miles of the city. The Sahel nomads need firewood too, and they have to burn dung which would otherwise fertilise the soil.

Jeremy Swift (1978) in a different context has advocated measures – not costly, not complicated, not calling for numbers of expert staff – that would actually help the Tuareg to tide over at least their usual shortage of the dry season. After a warning that nomads who are compelled to settle will suffer more than before in the dry season unless there is some provision for a supply of fodder, and that the cost of this, if it were to be done by irrigation, would be prohibitive, he suggests that simple methods of retaining rain-water, which are practised in other parts of the world, could be used so that fodder could be grown in stream-beds; that groups of herd owners could be given exclusive control over specified areas where they could set aside reserve pastures for the dry season; that herdsmen should be encouraged to diversify their stock rather than the reverse; and that facilities for both banking and credit could enable them to build up supplies of grain at the time when it is plentiful and cheap.

A problem that can arise in regions less susceptible to drought is competition for land between pastoralists and farmers. An example (Campbell, 1981) is on record from the Loitokitok area of Kenya, on the foothills of Mount Kilimanjaro, which was allotted to the Maasai as a reserve when in 1912 they were moved from their pastures further north to make land availble for alienation to Europeans. Today some Maasai are spontaneously taking up settled farming, but a greater number of Kikuyu cultivators from their own overcrowded former reserves have also migrated into Loitokitok. The movements of the herdsmen have further been limited by the creation of national parks which, if they are properly kept, can serve valuable ecological and economic ends: they protect from destruction the forests which are not only a direct economic asset but counter erosion by holding the soil; they protect animal species threatened with extermination, which have an important place in the ecology of the region; and – what concerns development planners most –they earn revenue from tourism. It is not for an anthropologist to decide between these rival uses for scarce land, but it would still be for him to urge that as much as possible ought to be learned about what is going on there. A British official once firmly announced that the Maasai must give up their 'pernicious pastoral proclivities'; but it is not as simple as that.

Farmers or Peasants?

Far more numerous than the pastoralists are the cultivators who are often referred to more or less loosely as peasants. This is a word well established in English, as are its equivalents in most European languages. Its basic connotation is of a man who gets his living by cultivating land that he does not own, and in recent years various definitions have been offered to indicate the precise nature of the limitations on his freedom that this implies. This definition would apply to the vast majority of tillers of the soil in Asia and still to a good many on the shores of the Mediterranean, but there are still many Africans who hold land on hereditary right, and some have become individual owners under laws enacted in the colonial period. Another definition disregards the question of dependent status and simply says that a peasant grows his own food but also sells a surplus or some inedible crop for which there is a market. This definition would certainly cover Africans. Perhaps it is in these terms that nomad pastoralists and even sometimes fishermen are classed along with peasants (for example by Firth in a book called *Malay Fishermen: Their Peasant Economy*). Writers have made generalizations about a 'peasant mentality' which is supposedly hostile to progress, and although they have admittedly based their observations on populations of peasants in the narrower sense, it may be that readers concerned with peasants in the wider may think their remarks are of general application.

But it is a great mistake to assume that all peasants are alike. They may have many different kinds of development problems and they may be organised in many different ways. Most of them suffer from shortage of water, and need to have it provided by irrigation or well-boring, or some of the simpler devices for retaining rainwater that may escape the development agent's notice. A few have more than enough rain, and their principal need is for protection against plant pests. Some plough with oxen, some with buffaloes, some simply turn up the soil with a cutlass or a stick. There are great differences in the variety of crafts that are practised and in the techniques of any one craft. The division of labour between men and women is very different in different societies. Both Islam and Hinduism hold that women should not be seen by men other than their husbands and close kin, and hence should not work in the fields; but there are very great differences in the degree to which this rule is observed in practice. In some African societies women may not go near cattle; in others only they may do the milking. The Swahili of Chole Island in Tanzania think women are too clumsy to do sewing. The Siane of the New Guinea Highlands think they are too stupid to handle axes.

But for an anthropologist the significant differences are in social structure, and in norms and values that may indeed sometimes engender resistance to beneficial innovations, but on the other hand, if they were better understood, might be harnessed to development policies instead of causing disillusion and disappointment. It is of such differences in social structure that a development agent most needs to be aware.

To begin with, the rules of inheritance and disposal of property may vary with the kinship system (see Chapter 3). Indeed, some anthropologists would say that the kinship system consists of these rules; in these terms, kinship systems differ widely. Kinship rules affect the question what members of a family or household actually receive the cash income that development is expected to generate, and decide how it should be laid out. A system of inheritance through women, in which a man's property, capital or savings, do not go to his own sons, although they are expected to work along with him, presents special problems. There are different rules as to the place where a couple should live when they are first married – near the husband's kin, near the wife's, or where they like. Such rules may affect the way in which working groups are formed. There are different rules about household property; sometimes spouses hold it in common, sometimes husband and wife have each their separate share. Different divorce rules make separation easier in some societies than in others; they may give a wife some initiative in the matter or none at all. Rules for the legitimacy of children affect people's claims to property. Muslims allow women to inherit, most other third world peoples do not.

The rules of landowning vary with other kinship rules, or access to land may not depend on kinship at all, but on allegiance to a political superior. The peasants of whom Eric Wolf writes are dependent on landlords; this is true over a great part of the world, but not of all those whom development is intended to help. Moreover, the terms on which land is allocated, and the possible relations between landlords and their dependents, also vary; a landlord may have his fields worked by people with whom he has a personal relationship or by casual daily-paid labour, and the terms of the relationship cannot be assumed to be the same in all cases.

Although nearly all the LDCs have passed through a period of colonial rule during which administrative authorities were imposed on them, most villagers still look to leaders who derive their legitimacy from a more distant past. These too may be of many kinds. The man to whom a village looks for leadership may be a ritual specialist or one who is temporarily ahead in a competition for lavishness in ceremonial exchanges, or one whose descent gives him a claim to it. Some form of collective leadership may be recognised, that of the older men as a body or of a council of lineage heads belonging to a dominant caste (but in these cases, however 'collective' the ideal, there will certainly be individuals who carry more influence than their fellows). There may be factional divisions in a village, so that two leaders are in competition and each calls on his followers to thwart the other's. Any such leader may be a source of support or obstruction to a development worker; if he is bypassed altogether, he may actively sabotage their work, or at the least reduce its effectiveness through mere passivity ('masterly inactivity' this is called by those who admire it).

There are differences in religious belief, though the adherents of any traditional religion are apt to have a conservative outlook in common. Whereas the religious specialists, who read and expound sacred books, are interested in the nature of the beings whom they worship and the ethical principles which these beings are believed to have laid down, the simple peasant is apt to look to religion primarily for an explanation of misfortunes or disasters. The religious explanation of disaster is that it is a punishment for sin, and any deviation from established ways may be interpreted as a sin. Natural disasters such as drought have sometimes been explained by the anger of the ancestors at the neglect of customs which do not have any particular moral significance but are just 'what was always done'.

The Indian caste system, which will be considered at more length in the discussion of equality and inequality (Chapter 6), rests ultimately on the ritual ranking of occupations according to the degree of polluting contacts which they involve. People whose occupation is not polluting are themselves polluted by contact with those of lower caste, and so must not eat with them. Hence members of a lower caste are debarred from social intercourse with their caste superiors, and – in the traditional system – from any economic co-operation except in the relationship of master and servant. In that system, the so-called 'untouchables' fell below a 'pollution line' which excluded them from all contact with members of 'clean castes', so that they had to live in separate quarters of a village and use separate wells, and were not allowed to enter the temples in which members of clean castes worshipped. These rules created a highly stratified society, but it is important to understand that the separation of higher from lower castes was not just a matter of snobbery. Pollution is a real danger to those who hold these religious beliefs. Under the influence of Gandhi and of modern somewhat more egalitarian ideas, discrimination against members of unclean castes has become a good deal less strict. Indeed it is now forbidden by law in India, but this does not by any means signify that it is never practised.

In some religions, the idea of an individual fate that one cannot escape may lead people to take little interest in plans to improve their fortunes. Hinduism and Islam both include such an idea, but it is very important to be aware how much or how little in a given case people's attitudes towards the practical problems of their own lives are affected by it. It is too easy to ascribe resistance or indifference to development projects to 'fatalism'. The belief may be temporarily forgotten; or there may be a way of getting round it, as there is with the Yoruba in Nigeria. They believe that everyone is endowed with a destiny at the moment of his birth; it may be good or bad. But there are ways of getting the better of a 'bad destiny', and even a good one may come to nothing if its holder does not bestir himself to make the most of it. Certainly the Yoruba have not been behindhand in economic activity. We need to learn more about the real effect of such beliefs on the everyday decisions of those who hold them.

Some religions, however, have been marked by attitudes very like those that are generally associated with Protestant Christianity and its insistence on hard work, frugal living, and thrift. Capitalist economies developed in Europe during the period of the Reformation, though it was not only Protestant countries which took part in the development. Elsewhere, the adherents of such religions of austerity have sometimes been ahead of their neighbours in taking advantage of the capitalist system that was brought to them from outside. In Java the organisation of retail trade on a capitalist basis was the work of a reformist Muslim movement which not only valued austerity but insisted on the duty of making the pilgrimage to Mecca. It was that duty, a costly one, that drove the members of this sect to practise thrift.

In Africa the adherents of particular Christian sects or of independent African churches have sometimes shown a particular aptitude for business dealings. Norman Long (1968) has described the economic success of the Jehovah's Witnesses in Zambia, where they have been found particularly trustworthy. A more recent study (Barrett, 1979) shows how in Olowo, a Yoruba fishing village, a community founded by a prophet was described when it had been in existence for only four years as the most successful example of village-level development in Nigeria. It bought an electricity generator, established some small factories, set up a river transport service and invested in ocean-going trawlers. The people, who numbered perhaps about a thousand, had all property in common and worked in groups under the direction of leaders; those who were lazy were flogged and given no food. A section of the community seceded after a few years because they resented this close control, but they did not achieve any comparable economic development. It is important to notice that the communal system was not created or maintained by any democratic movement. Decisions were taken and imposed by the leaders, and it was they who made the business calculations, and evidently made them successfully; we cannot be sure that they owed their business success to their religious beliefs. A people who have no particular religious belief to inspire them, the Tolai in New Guinea, are conspicuous for their interest in production for the market. We should remember too that all the attempts that have been made to identify societies particularly well disposed towards development have been looking for entrepreneurs, people good at recognizing profitable opportunities and acting upon the belief that they can succeed. Many of the new states reject the values of capitalism and base their hopes on various interpretations of socialism; they prize equality above originality (see Chapter 4). In such states, entrepreneurship is more likely to be used in circumventing imposed controls than on lines approved by the authorities.

The Legacy of Colonial Rule

Not only the current drive for development but the whole process of European expansion has had an element of historical accident, in the sense that Western technology was brought to peoples whose own technical equipment and political organisation were of very different types. Despite the changes that have been made under western influence, whether through colonial rule or in other ways, these differences still persist, as this chapter has sought to show; but the makers of development plans generally show little awareness of them.

In India, Sri Lanka and Indonesia we see the heirs of empires that go back hundreds of years further than the British or the Dutch. Africa too has had its empires, though on a smaller scale. In these empires there was a well-established hierarchy, with a chain of command from capital to village, and along with it went, as it commonly does, wide differences in wealth. Many crafts were practised, and there was considerable internal trade. In such a polity it may be possible to effect changes in the behaviour of a great number of people by securing the agreement of those who hold power; indeed this was the aim of many colonial rulers, particularly when they were trying to bring about what they conceived as improvements in ways of life and standards of living. On the other hand, if what is sought is the reduction of inequalities in wealth, the traditional holders of power are likely to oppose measures with that intention. In most of the new states, the older rulers themselves have been replaced at the summit by the leaders of political parties. But there are still power-holders lower down the scale, notably large landowners, who can block attempts at redistribution.

In those parts of Africa where soils are poor and mineral resources could not be exploited before modern machinery was introduced, there were no large political units, and no conspicuously rich rulers. The interior of New Guinea knew no metal instruments until the 1930s, a fact which has led superficial observers to call the inhabitants 'Stone Age people', as if they lived like the prehistoric men whom archaeologists study. They recognised no permanent authority, but they appreciated differences in wealth, and readily engaged in development in the form of coffee planting.

People subject to colonial rule are dependent in the sense that policies are made for them, and often without much attention to their views. Colonial rulers may be paternalistic in that they try, even if misguidedly, to make their rule benevolent, or they may be pure exploiters; any particular instance will be described in one way or the other according to the values of the person judging it. But, in more than one sense, the economy of colonial territories has been dependent on that of their rulers. The local populations have often been required to produce quotas of specified crops; and although most of them now take wage labour for granted, in the beginning many were directly or indirectly forced to work in employment centres. Opinions differ as to the extent to which the economies of former colonial territories are still dependent on those of the rich countries.

Colonial rule has certainly left behind it other forms of dependence than the strictly economic. No colonial power was markedly generous in the provision that it made for education, though some increased it considerably as the time for political independence was seen to be near. As a result, the number of highly educated people who are qualified to make or advise on development plans has been largely a matter of the length of time during which colonial rule was maintained. This was longer in India, Sri Lanka and Indonesia than in other parts of the developing world. In Africa and in most of the Pacific, it has been impossible to do without imported expert advice, and this has often come from nationals of the former ruling power, if only because theirs is the language that the educated minority have learnt. The French made technical assistance agreements with nearly all their former colonies, under which they provided most of the experts needed. In the educational field the consequence has been that secondary and higher education in francophone Africa is still directed to the examinations held in France. (But this kind of intellecutal dependence can exist even where there is no foreign presence; some schools in India still do sums in pounds, shillings and pence, though these units were not used in India even at the time when they were in Britain.) Some new states have engaged expert advisers from a variety of countries so as to avoid dependence on any one; that strategy sometimes had the disadvantage that the experts could not agree on the kind of advice to offer.

In later chapters I propose to discuss in more detail those aspects of the social structure and culture of the LDCs which anyone engaged in planning or monitoring a development project would particularly have to take into account.

3

Family and Kinship

All the world over, people live in families, and development planning accepts this as a basic fact. When the land of large estates is redistributed, the holdings are supposedly calculated to be sufficient to support a family, sometimes with a surplus beyond bare essentials. When populations have to be re-settled – because their homes have been flooded when a dam was built, or destroyed by an earthquake, or perhaps because they are refugees – the authorities aim to produce family housing. Wages may be set in relation to the supposed needs of a family – though, indeed, it has often been thought that there need be only enough to keep a single man, on the assumption that the family he had left at home could look after itself.

When accurate censuses were not taken, populations were often estimated by counting the adult males, the number of whom could be got from tax registers, and multiplying the result by a figure assumed to represent average family size. In Tanganyika under British administration this figure was 4.5. From the 1967 census in Tanzania it was calculated that the average woman in that country bears 6.6 children in the course of her life. But we would still want to know how many children died in infancy before we could begin to talk about average family size.

Types of Family

But there are many more questions to ask about families besides the number of children a woman bears. And indeed the first question is what different societies consider a family to be. We agree that it is a domestic unit, a group of people living and keeping house together. What is called the *nuclear*, or some-times the *elementary*, family consists of an adult couple with their children. Such a group need not have the legal status that is given it by the marriage of the parents; if it does, we may call it the *simple legal family*. Marriage rules may allow a man to have more than one wife (polygyny); in that case the family will consist of the father, two or more mothers and their children. This has been described as a number of simple legal families linked by a common father (Evans-Pritchard, 1951, p. 108). Sons may continue to live at their father's residence after they are themselves husbands and fathers, as has been the custom in India and China. In India this arrangement is called the *joint family*. When there was no wage employment outside the village and everyone got subsistence from the land (either by working it directly or by employing others to work it), the whole harvest of the owning family's land was pooled, and the head of the household decided how much should be given to dependents (see Chapter 4), how much kept for the next sowing and how much divided among his sons and *their* families. In Japan and Malaysia the traditional family consisted of a couple, their unmarried children and one adult child; in Japan it was always a son, in Malaysia it might be a daughter. The child who stayed at home had to look after the parents when they grew old, and would eventually inherit the dwelling. In much of Africa, married sons continue to live near their father or actually in his homestead while they farm their own portion of the group's land and support their own families from it; such an organization is called the *extended family*. Mediterranean and Latin American peasants are Christian and live in nuclear families.

Every individual recognises kin who are linked to him through both his parents, and expects to claim friendship and assistance from any of them who live near him. But in many societies the claim to a share of group property, which rests on *descent*, is derived from one parent only. A property-holding group based on descent so limited is called a *unilineal descent group* (sometimes UDG) or *lineage*. If descent is traced from father to son, and this is by far the most common rule, it is called *patrilineal*. A patrilineal extended family is a three-generation lineage together with the spouses of the men, and without the women, who will have married into other lineages. The incoming spouses, though they are members of the family, are not members of the lineage; lineage is given at birth and is changed only in exceptional circumstances.

Matrilineal descent is traced from mother to son. It is found mainly in regions with poor resources, where there is not much possibility of accumulating property, so that claims to inheritance are of little significance. But there are one or two striking exceptions to this generalization. The matrilineal Akanspeaking peoples of Ghana are the world's biggest producers of cocoa. By an odd coincidence, the matrilineal Tolai of New Britain are also successful cocoa-growers. The matrilineal Nayars of the three states of south-west India that are now united in Kerala, were until recently the dominant land-owning caste of that region. Matriliny is also found in a belt of territory stretching across Africa through Zaire, Zambia, Malawi and Tanzania. It is important to realise that although women are formally the owners of lineage property and sometimes have a say in the disposal of it, they do not exercise any more authority than they do in patrilineal societies. Their brothers take the lineage decisions. So, although a man's property is derived from his mother, the property itself comes to him from his mother's brother. And since, though he has only one father, he may have several mother's brothers, he and his cousins have claims on the property of a number of men, supposing they have property worth claiming. Matrilineal systems are rather difficult to understand for people who are not used to them.

There are also societies in which people regard their kin on both father's and mother's side as equally important. When a new household is set up by marriage, both husband and wife get a share of the property of both their parents. Such societies have been described by a variety of terms, among them *nonunilineal, bilateral* and *ambilineal.* They are most commonly found in Malaysia and the Philippines.

One of the most striking consequences of economic development, which began long before development was deliberately planned, is that the family is no longer a unit for purposes of production. Different members can now find employment on their own initiative, and then they may or may not contribute their earnings to a common family pool. Very rarely does a young man let his father decide what he should do with his wages; indeed if he is working at a distant centre, he will inevitably have spent some part of them on mere subsistence before he comes home, and he will most likely buy himself smart clothes, a wrist-watch, a guitar, or a transistor, as well. Old men complain that young men have lost respect for their elders; but at this point in time, every old man who talks like that has been a young wage-earner in his day. In fact the wage-earners do bring money or presents home, or they send money orders now that postal facilities are provided; and they seek employment not for pocket-money but to build up the farm at home.

But one consequence of the new employments is that the wage-earner knows just how much his work is worth – and whether his brothers are earning as much as he is. In an Indian joint family the one who earns most may not like to see his wages shared with the rest, and this has been a reason for brothers in many families to want the family land to be partitioned earlier than they used to. According to F. G. Bailey, the result in the village of Bisipara in Orissa, where he worked, was that farms became too small to produce any margin to meet emergencies, and so had to be sold; they were sold to men with business interests who wanted to raise their status by becoming landowners. Hence the Warrior caste, which originally owned nearly all the land of the village, lost much of its influence (Bailey, 1957).

The general trend towards independent employment has led observers to suppose that the Indian joint family is ceasing to exist. But closer attention shows that the group of father and adult sons (what in Africa would be called a minimal lineage) have not everywhere repudiated their mutual obligations; they simply fulfil them in a different way. Scarlett Epstein calls the new grouping the *share family*. According to her, in the village of Dalena, with its diversified economy, related nuclear families, each with its own source of income, 'agreed to share the responsibility for their incomes as well as for their expenditure' (1973, p. 207). In this way farming brothers share with wage-earners; the latter keep their land in the village, the former work it and send some of the harvest to the brother in town. He in turn provides them with the cash they need. Similarly some urban families in Meerut, in north India, keep in close contact with the rural kin with whom they would once have formed a joint family, and recognise the authority of the senior man living in the country. They seek his approval for any unusual expenditure, and for plans for the education and employment of the younger members. In this case few urban families are able to help their rural brothers. More often they keep up their rights in the land so as to have a claim on its produce; many urban families depend on this (Vatuk, 1972, pp. 129–33).

Special Problems of Matriliny

Where inheritance is matrilineal, special difficulties have arisen as new opportunities have made it possible to acquire property from sources outside the descent group. This problem has been most acute in the cases where the lineage is a land-holding group, that is in the exceptional cases where matrilineal peoples occupy productive land. We mentioned that the Akan-speaking peoples of Ghana live in the cocoa-producing rain-forest area, and many of them have done very well out of cocoa. When this crop was found to be profitable, many men planted new land; by the rules of matrilineal descent this should have become part of the property that they shared with their sisters, and have been divided between these women's children when they died. But a cocoa farmer, or any other farmer, works or manages a farm with his own sons, not his sisters' sons, and they are close to him in a way that his nephews are not; he is apt to want to set them up in life by leaving the new farm to them, and they on their side are apt to think that that is only a fair return for the work they have put in. Naturally the nephews take a different view; they want him to follow the recognised rule. Tolai men, even before they took up cocoa, had their own way of getting round the rules. A man who had made a success in trade, and acquired the great coils of shell money that used to be their currency, would bury them somewhere and keep the place a secret from his lineage kin, so that they would not be found and distributed when he died; he would let his sons know so that they could dig them up later.

A compromise that has often been found is to agree that 'self-acquired' or 'individual' property is at the disposal of the man who has acquired it, so that he can leave it to his own children. But after that it is merged in their descent-group property and passes on in the female line. This solution was adopted in Kerala, where the Nayars were the first to be educated, and so to earn incomes from other sources than farm work and invest their money in land, with which they endowed their wives and children (Fuller, 1976, p. 131).

The crucial problem for matrilineal systems has been the balance between the claims made on a person (man or woman) by siblings on the one hand and spouse on the other. A mother is devoted to her children's interests, but still she must think of her duty to her lineage kin. A father should not in theory think of his children's interests at all; they are not members of his lineage. Elizabeth Colson (1958) has shown what kinds of conflict arise in the families of prosperous Plateau Tonga farmers in Zambia, or indeed those of younger men who are working for wages to set up farms. The rules almost seem to require enmity between husband and wife, in which, of course, the sons should side with their mothers. Some mothers encourage their sons to get as much as they can out of their father while he is alive, since they will get nothing when he dies; and the sons may think this is how they make sure of a return for the work they do. A young man who is asked to do some business in town for his father may cheat him; or he may simply refuse to work on the farm. As for the young wage-earner, if he brings presents home for his father his lineage kin may be angry; Colson quotes a case when such a young man died, and they were thought to have killed him by sorcery. And another young man, who wanted to be a good son, and whose mother wanted him to, was afraid of sorcery from his mother's kin.

In Ghana a study of marriage among the salaried élite in the capital tells us something about the difficulties of women in the most westernized section of a matrilineal society. Here most women earn money, for different reasons. Of course there is always an advantage in having some financial independence. But it may be also that a husband's income is not enough to support his nuclear family because of his obligations to his descent-group kin, particularly if he is the only well-to-do member of that group. A reason that weighs with most women is that they may find themselves destitute if a husband dies and his kin take all his property. Both spouses may want to build a house for retirement, but they do not often do this as a joint venture; more often the woman will start a small business in partnership with her mother, and depend on what she saves from that. If the wife's kin come to visit, it is usually to help in the house; but the husband's kin may come to help themselves to the food in the fridge or 'borrow' his car or his television set (Oppong, 1974).

Why does a system persist when it creates such difficulties? Partly because the numbers of people who stand to gain from their father's or their uncles' property are about equal, and the latter stand up for the old system. Among the urban minority, ideas may change as the younger recruits to it are further from their rural background.

Female-headed Families

The *female-headed* family is a type of domestic unit produced by modern conditions; it has no counterpart in any pre-industrial tradition. There have, of course, often been families whose male head was absent, sometimes because he had taken service in an army or been conscripted, more often because he had gone to work for wages somewhere away from home. Migrant labour is older than colonial rule, but its extent increased very greatly during the colonial period; Chinese and Indians, and men from the Pacific Islands, were recruited by fair means or foul, and always on long-term contracts, to work in places many miles by sea from their homes – Pacific Islanders on the sugar plantations of Queensland, Chinese on the sugar plantations of Natal, Indians to build railways in East Africa, to mention only a few examples. Later the mining areas of southern and central Africa drew their labour force from distant parts of the continent; at first these workers too were constrained by long-term contracts which it was a criminal offence to break, but as time went on a period of spontaneous migration came to be taken for granted as a part of every man's life. There was similar migration from the Caribbean Islands to the United States, and indeed from Ireland to England. Since the end of the Second World War there has been large-scale migration of labour from the poorer to the richer European countries, perhaps to be seen at its most striking when peasants from southern France are found working on the oil rigs in the North Sea.

All these movements leave families temporarily without a father, but the families are not fatherless. The mothers take on additional responsibilities; they may be able to rely for help and protection on other men of their husband's family; if a man sends money home – and this after all is what he has gone away for – his wife can pay someone to do heavy work for her; one does not find communities where all the men are away at the same time.

In those societies where a woman is not expected to be always under the guardianship of some man, she may become the head of a household through being widowed or separated from her husband. But in these days one can sometimes find a household consisting of a woman with her daughters and their children, none of whom have been married. Such households do not represent any older tradition; they are wholly the product of modern conditions. They have been observed principally in Caribbean countries, and their existence has often been accounted for by the assumption that the peoples of those countries are sexually promiscuous and their men have no sense of responsibility towards their children or the mothers of those children.

R. T. Smith (1956) showed from a study made in (then) British Guiana that it is largely because men have so strong a sense of responsibility towards their own mothers that they cannot always support the mothers of their own children. It is true that no stigma attaches to conception before marriage, but it is also true that the ideal is for a couple who have children to live together; and if they do, the man is expected to maintain his wife, and their children until they are old enough to earn. But he is often away from home working for wages; he is never the head of a productive team, as is the father of a farming family; his children do not depend on him for a share in a patrimony that they will inherit. When he is at home he exerts authority and expects deference, but the mother is the actual manager of the household, and as soon as the sons begin earning they bring their wages to her. By this time she is in a position to earn money herself, either by petty trading or in some kinds of unskilled labour, and if her husband dies or leaves her she is supported by such activities and by her sons. Many a man cannot both maintain his mother and support a household, though most of them contribute something to the maintenance of any children that they may have.

Many a man may have to wait to set up his own household until his mother dies. In the meantime, no doubt he will have children and will contribute what he can to their support. Both young men and girls may have children by a number of partners before they form a permanent relationship (called a 'common law' marriage if it is not entered upon with legal formalities). In such a relationship the man may accept the woman's 'outside children', but if he does not she leaves them with her mother. But some woman never enter any common law or legal marriage, and live all their lives in their mother's house.

Although some children are the offspring of casual encounters, it is clear that there are recognised norms of marital and parental responsibility. Why then should so many families be set up without the foundation of legal marriage? Smith answers this question by considering what are the circumstances in which legal marriage and legitimate paternity are important. In the first place, where there is property to inherit, claims to a share of it rest on legitimate descent. Second, a man who is socially mobile takes with him his legally recognized dependents but not others. It is in the lowest social stratum of Caribbean society that one finds the prevalence of common law marriage (although there too legal marriage is the ideal). Here there is practically no heritable property, and there are practically no opportunities for social mobility; hardly anyone can rise above the level of an unskilled labourer. The only leader in the village is the school teacher, and he stands for the norms of the wider society and does make a legal marriage. Others who have ambitions and a chance of realizing them leave the village for some employment in town.

Again, the male ideal makes the father the authority in the home and the sole support of his wife and young children; and this is the female ideal of legal marriage too. But though a father expects to be obeyed and respected when he is there, he is so often absent that real authority and the making of decisions must rest with the mother; and on her side, she is aware that, once she is no longer handicapped by young children, her employment opportunities are as good as his. A woman has as good a chance as a man of owning a house, and when she does she naturally considers herself to be its head.

A somewhat similar situation was observed among people born in the slum area of an urban location in East London, South Africa (Pauw, 1963). Forty-six households in a sample of 109 had female heads, and nearly a quarter of these heads were unmarried mothers. These were younger women; those over 40 claimed to have been married at some time. Whether married or not, their dependents were unmarried children and the children of unmarried daughters. Pauw is writing of a population with a strong tradition of patriliny, of patrilineal descent as the basis of inheritance claims to land and cattle, to political office and to rank in a markedly hierarchical society. In such a society, legally recognized marriage as the basis of legitimate descent is crucial. But traditions of this kind are not carried over into contexts where they are meaningless. In East London – and its successor, the new township of Mdantsane in the 'Bantu homeland' – the illiterate population which has lost its roots in the country, like that in Guyana, has nothing to inherit and no possibility of rising above the ranks of unskilled labour. In the new township there are more lucrative employments than before, and increasing numbers of leadership positions as a limited local autonomy is granted to the African areas, but these are for the literate, and the literate are sticklers for legal marriage and – at least in appearance – strict rules of sexual morality, as are their counterparts in Guyana.

In the former British territories in the Caribbean, a man is legally bound to support his children whether he is married to their mother or not, but of course if he fails to do so it is not always easy for her to enforce this claim. The question how much hardship is caused by men's neglect of their children is a matter of subjective impressions where no detailed observations have been made. As Smith's study shows, many people in Guyana are very poor, and he argues that the attitudes towards marriage and paternity are a feature of this poverty; but he stresses the point that, at the level at which the people of his

Guyanese villages were living, women could do as well for themselves as men as long as they were not handicapped by young children, and at the time when they were, there was usually someone to contribute to their support. More recently a series of village discussions ('workshops' as it is now fashionable to call them) organised in Jamaica by the Women's Bureau of the Prime Minister's Office, reported that there was 'a general pattern of unsupportive fathers'. But their conclusion that it was 'necessary to re-educate the whole society so that both sexes have equal responsibility in maintaining the family' is a statement of an ideal rather than a guide to practical action (Indian Council of Social Science Research, 1978, pp. 62–3).

The Family Dwelling

The organisation of living space in the family dwelling is an aspect of its life that cannot be taken for granted. It differs greatly from one society to another. In an African extended family, polygynous or not, every married woman (wives of the head and his brothers and sons) traditionally had her own quarters where she and her young children lived. They formed a recognised sub-unit in the total family, and property was allotted to them, or inherited by them, as a unit (the house-property complex, a use of the word that has nothing to do with Freud).

A detailed account of the lay-out of such a family dwelling among the Tallensi of northern Ghana, at a time when that area was very little developed, has been given by Fortes (1949). A Tale homestead consists of a number of separate huts (Fortes calls them 'rooms') built of dried mud with thatched roofs, the whole surrounded by a mud wall. It is entered by a narrow gate which can be closed at night to keep out thieves or marauding animals. Immediately inside the gate is the space for the livestock, and opening on this is a hut where the ancestor spirits of the homestead head (and so of all male members) are believed to have their abode, and where his funeral rites will be performed. The men of the family, when they are at home, sit outside the gate under a shade tree. The public, masculine part of the homestead is divided from the domestic part by a low wall, and in the middle of this wall is the tall granary where the harvest from the family fields is stored. It is under the sole authority of the homestead head, and nobody may take grain from it without his permission; but he is expected to distribute it among the women with absolute impartiality. Behind the wall are the women's quarters, each a collection of huts and a courtyard. Each woman has a living hut, a kitchen and a store. Here she sleeps with her young children and cooks for them and her husband, and is visisted by—for example—her daughters' suitors, after, of course, they have confronted the homestead head. The senior wife keeps her husband's property here.

The mother of the homestead head is the senior woman of the whole group and has the largest courtyard. His senior wife has quarters on her right; on her left is a second wife of the head, or else the senior wife of his next younger brother. There is no fixed order for additional women, who in an extended family include the wives of the head's sons. Finally there is a grinding hut, in a large homestead sometimes more than one, where grain is ground by the different wives, each by herself.

A very different structure is the 'long-house' of Borneo and Sarawak, in which a number of separate but generally somehow related families live literally side by side. The long-house is a single structure which may extend for sixty to a hundred yards, standing on piles on a river-bank, approached by ladders which lead to an open platform, then a covered gallery, and then a line of separate rooms. In each of these lives a family of parents and children, and it is their total living space. One adult child – it may be either a son or a daughter – should live permanently with the parents, bringing his or her spouse to join them; the others move out. A couple attach themselves where they choose and are welcomed; this would be in any long-house where they have kin, and there they are allotted, or build on, a room where they will cook, eat, sleep and keep their property. They also control a section of the gallery, though this is normally treated as a public space. The dwellers in a long-house recognise the authority of a headman, who can intervene to settle disputes, for example in the division of property when a son or daughter moves out to live elsewhere. As Freeman

(1958) remarks, the long-house is more like a village in which there are a number of nuclear families, most of them related by some link of kinship, just as one found in villages everywhere in the days when travel was limited to the distance one could go on foot.

An Indian joint family may be really joint in the sense that the component nuclear families do not have separate living quarters. A detailed account of life in such a family in Mysore was written very recently (Hobson, 1978). The house described stood in a street, with a narrow space between it and the next. All the women slept in one room, each on a rush mat with her children around her, and all the men in another, the room where they also ate. In the floor of this room was a sunken area where those who needed ritual purification *must* wash, and anyone could; any women might wash any of the children. Each woman kept her personal possessions in a locked box in the sleeping room. The women took it in turns to cook in the one kitchen, but all shared in the preparation of food, notably grinding and pounding. The head's wife kept them at it and assigned tasks when this was necessary. There was a common store-room for domestic utensils and another for farming ones; next to it was a space where the animals slept. In this stifling proximity, people who had quarrelled had refused to speak to one another for a year or more. When the joint family divided, as it did shortly after the time of this description, every type of property down to plates and tumblers was distributed in supposedly equal shares, and the house space was divided; the account does not explain how.

A feminine view of joint-family living is expressed in a marriage song recorded by Berreman (1972), in which the bride's pretended bargaining with her new affines includes demands for 'a separate fireplace' and 'a separate big house'.

A different type of house is that sometimes built for a wealthy joint family in Gujarat (Pocock, 1972). In such a house there is a separate door for each of the component families, and it is built so that, if the joint family divides, each can have its own hearth and bathing place. While it is undivided there are connecting doors between the sections and only one hearth is used for cooking; when it divides the doors are sealed up.

Family Rituals

Much religious activity centres in the family. Important rituals mark the passage of an individual through life, and whatever other roles he may fill, a normal individual will be a child in one family (the family of *orientation*) and a parent in another (the family of *procreation*). All these rituals are the direct concern of family and kin, whoever else may attend them. Indeed it is a remarkable fact that in the most secularised of modern societies, most people still think that crucial stages in their own or their children's lives ought to be marked by ritual or at least solemnised. They still celebrate marriages and mourn deaths, and many people follow the rites of an organised church on these occasions. Some, probably fewer, such people also seek a blessing – in the Christian church in the form of baptism – on newly born children. The feeling that these crucial moments need to be marked by reference to some transcendent power holds sway even over people who do not believe that there is any such power.

The entry on adult life, marriage, the birth of children and death, are the occasions for such ritual. We enumerate them in this order because it is adults who ritualise the birth of a child. The birth of a first child is what makes people parents, and until the child is a good deal older, it is they who nourish hopes and fears for its future.

The class of ritual associated with these events has been called by many names. Van Gennep, the anthropologist who first recognised it as forming a special category, introduced the term (in French) *rites de passage*, a phrase later translated as 'rites of passage' or 'passage rituals'. Some writers use the term 'life-crisis rituals'; this refers to the fact that they mark critical periods in an individual's life, but perhaps too readily suggests that these are times of crisis in the sense of impending disaster. Another possible phrase is 'transition ritual'.

The transition in question is that from one social status to another; at each stage the whole community, represented sometimes by a political authority, sometimes by the family and kin group, confers on an individual his appropriate standing. An infant does not become a member of society simply by being born; indeed there are societies in which an infant who dies before the birth ritual has been performed is not considered to have lived. Many societies prepare young people for adult life by an elaborate process of initiation; this makes children into adults, and it incorporates them into a neighbourhood group, wider than the family which has been the focus of their relationships up to that point. By making children adult, initiation makes them marriageable; in the case of girls it may be combined with the ritual of marriage. Where this is not done, marriage is a ritual by itself, and is in fact considered to be what makes the couple fully adult. We have noted that the birth of their first child makes a couple parents and completes the family, and birth ritual is often focused on the mother. A death, for the person who dies, is a transition from membership of the living community to the status of an ancestor, one of the dead who are held to be still associated with their living descendants. If the mortuary ritual is not performed, or is incorrectly performed, the spirit, it is thought, will not go to the place of the ancestors but will haunt the living and bring misfortunes upon them. A death also causes a rearrangement of relationships among the living; a successor to the dead person must be installed in his place, and his property distributed. Widows, heirs, successors are all going through a change of status too.

Van Gennep pointed out that the person who is the central figure in such a ritual is first separated from his society, next passes a period of time in isolation and then returns in his new status. The transition period may be one of formal preparation for the new role; it is conspicuously so in ceremonies of initiation, sometimes also at marriage. Or it may simply mark a break between the person's departure in one role and return in another. This is called the *liminal* stage, the period 'on the threshold' neither in nor out, 'betwixt and between' as Turner (1967, pp. 93ff) has called it. Thus a mother (with her child) is often placed in seclusion after a birth; boys at initiation move to a camp built outside the village where uninitiated persons must not see them; brides (but not bridegrooms) are secluded before marriage.

All these rituals, then, take at least some of the participants away from their everyday activities, and they are liable to be very much curtailed if people whose presence is necessary cannot get leave from an employer on whom they depend for some, if not all, of their income.

In India every man has ritual responsibilities to the god of his household, which he must perform daily or weekly, and his wife must be present. This ritual unity of the couple, which is initiated at their marriage, is the reason why members of higher castes hold that a widow should not marry again. Educated reformers have opposed this rule for more than a century. But it may never have been followed by the lower castes.

4

Land Rights, Land Reform, Land Improvement

Plans to increase agricultural productions have two sides: the technical, which covers the improvement of water supplies and the adoption of high-yielding varieties of crop and the fertilizers, pesticides, and so on, on which the high yields depend, and the legal, that is the rules determining the cultivator's access to the land. The latter question, the one on which anthropologists have something to say, has both moral and technical aspects. Very many people consider that a farmer has a moral right to the land that he tills and that nobody should own land that he does not work himself. Others, perhaps not so many, assume that the way to stimulate the technical improvement is to make it easy to buy and sell land by allocating it to individuals who have sole control over the disposal of it. The latter course, it is argued, enables progressive farmers to buy up land from which inefficient farmers have been unable to make a living. What happens to the inefficient farmers? Often they work for wages, or on some other type of contract, on the same land as before. The two principles clearly cannot both be followed at the same time. A number of countries have followed first one and then the other.

There is also the view that small farmers' holdings should be pooled and worked collectively, again advocated in the interests both of justice and efficiency. Various countries, notably in the socialist world, have first followed this principle and then abandoned or modified it.

Traditional Land Rights

Where there is no great pressure of population on the land, rights to it depend upon inheritance, and everyone has a claim to inherit land somewhere. As was indicated in the preceding chapter, it may be inherited in the male line (father to son) or the female (a man to his sister's sons), or from both parents, or from one or other at will.

Unilineal inheritance (through one or other parent) is typical of Africa and India, Japan and China; cognatic inheritance (through both or either) is found in many parts of Malaysia and Indonesia. In such systems, claims may pass from an individual family through the son or daughter who chooses to live in the parents' house, as happens among the Iban of Borneo (Freeman, 1958) or, when a couple marry, both partners may be endowed with land by either parent at the time. A rule often found is that claims may be asserted by anyone descended in any way from the ancestor who originally held the land; the validity of this claim may be contested, but if it is successfully upheld the claimant cannot be refused land. The process was studied in detail among the Amhara of Ethiopia before their Marxist revolution (Hoben, 1973).

Where entitlement depends on membership of a unilineal (bounded) group, there is always the possibility that someone's share of the property may not be adequate to give him the level of subsistence that he thinks necessary, and there are always arrangements whereby a right-holder may admit an outsider to unused land, with the approval of the right-holding group's authorities; this is normally the only way in which these authorities may intervene in the decisions of individual right-holders. Thus we can distinguish between use-rights and property-rights (hundreds of other pairs of words have been devised to indicate this distinction). The former are granted at the will of holders of the latter; the holder of a use-right cannot dispose of it. As long as cultivation is predominantly for subsistence, the recipient of a use-right is not required to make any payment for it; at this level of development, such persons are commonly kinsmen of the right-holder from outside his lineage, and they often marry women of the right-holding group.

When some single descent-group establishes political dominance over an area wider than that which it claims as its own patrimony, and takes over responsibility for the maintenance of order within it, the head (now a king or chief) levies a tribute on the produce of the land, out of which he maintains his subordinate authorities (at a standard which raises their lifestyle above the general average, even if only a little). The representatives of political authority now assert the ultimate right to admit or refuse newcomers. But they still do not become landlords; they do not make contracts for rent, and the farmer who does not disobey his chief can expect to be undisturbed.

Although the members of a right-holding group commonly assert the principle that their land can never pass out of its possession, in fact payment begins to be offered for land wherever there is competition for it, and such transactions come to be recognized as sales as they would with any other commodity. They become more and more common as a commercial economy develops. Some colonial rulers have sought to regularize the process by the issue of titles to land and the establishment of a register of transactions, and this has sometimes had the effect of turning political authorities responsible for the collection of revenue into landlords with power to evict their tenants. This was the consequence of British policy in India, while in Ceylon (Sri Lanka) only land in actual occupation was registered, and the remaining large area claimed by the Crown and made available for plantation development. In Buganda, at a time when commercial agriculture was hardly known, political authorities were given freehold rights over large areas described as 'the estates of which they are already in possession'. Both in India and Ceylon policy was later directed to the protection of tenants; in Ceylon this shift took place only when independence was near. Nevertheless, one consequence of the earlier policy in India was that some former revenue collectors – *zamindars* – have been able, mainly through buying up one another's land, to build up large commercial farms which supply the bulk of grain sold in the towns. In Buganda, though the policy did create the status of tenants dependent on landlords, the initial reaction to the grant of very large areas was for the new owners to sell off portions of them, so that, although great inequalities remained, the number of owners increased considerably.

But the creation of individual rights was not the only way to reduce the cultivators to dependence on landlords. This has also been done where land was made available for alienation to immigrants and the indigenous inhabitants were excluded from it, not necessarily, or even usually, being removed from where they were actually living; more often they were confined within boundaries beyond which they could not expand as their numbers grew or they wanted to plant cash crops. The redistribution of alienated land has had a high priority for independent African governments.

In general, peasants who have little land, or none at all, work on other men's land on one of three possible arrangements. They may earn a daily or weekly wage. They may pay a rent which is a proportion either of the cash return for their produce or a share of the produce itself. Or they may make an agreement to work an area with contributions from the owner – seeds, manure or other fertilizer, draught animals for ploughing or threshing; this is called share-cropping. Whether any such agreement is oppressive depends on the relative bargaining power of the parties. Certainly the labourer is commonly the weaker, but this is not always so.

While the makers of development policies generally regard contracts to pay wages on the one hand or rent on the other as rational transactions, they condemn share-cropping agreements not only because they may be exploitative but also because they are assumed to be inherently inefficient. Tenants, they argue, have no incentive to work productively and landlords none to improve their property. This may well be true in many cases. Yet some anthropologists have recently observed that share-cropping stubbornly persists among the most diverse societies, and this can only be because tenants as well as landlords see advantages in it. One such advantage is that when a tenant receives a fixed share of a food crop, this is worth more when prices are high. It is not, of course, denied that many share-cropping agreements are extremely hard on the peasant.

Share-cropping

An anthropologist, A. W. Johnson (1971), has studied the type of contract made on a *fazenda* (the Portuguese word) in Brazil;

peasants there moved freely from one estate to another and were sometimes even enticed away by rival landowners. The *morador* (resident on the estate) was entitled to farm as much land as he could reasonably be expected to work, and could indicate the area he wanted to clear, though this was for the landlord to decide. He could cut firewood for his own use, and he was given seed for cotton, the cash crop. A man who had cleared land and established a crop, if he was evicted, had to be paid for the labour he had put in. The landlord decided what kind of contract to offer. Men who lived near the manager and could be easily supervised had to give two days' work a week, that is a third of their time; in addition the landlord took a third of the cotton crop and a third of the manioc flour (the staple food). Others were share-croppers in the strict sense, giving a third of their beans, maize, manioc flour and cotton, but keeping the whole yield of various other crops and distributing their time as they pleased. Their 'share' consisted in a house, a patch of land for their own subsistence, and manure from the landlord's cattle which grazed their land after harvest (and which might be let in early so that part of the harvest was lost). The landlord saw *his* share not as a part of the peasant's produce, but as part of a wage paid in kind.

Although such arrangements only provide the peasants with a very low standard of living, they regard them, says Johnson, as a form of exchange between equals. 'They cannot, of course, demand everything they wish from their patrons, but they can and do demand respect and fair play . . . . The workers expect to be treated courteously and fairly by the landlord, and will leave if he offends them' (1971, p. 130). No such personal relationship exists for workers at a fixed wage. Indeed, in many parts of the world landlords are coming to prefer wage labour just for this reason.

Another anthropologist, A. F. Robertson, working with an economist, F. Bray (1980), found in the state of Kelantan in Malaysia that share-cropping arrangements bring together families at the stage of their development when there are too many dependents to subsist on land to which they have rights with others – typically elderly couples or sick persons – who control more land than they are able to work. If the rice crop is to be successful, the various processes of cultivation must be timed to coincide over a wide area, and no land must be left untilled to be invaded by weeds. Share-cropping contracts, always for only a few years, 'marry' surplus land with surplus labour. Often they are made between kinsmen, and sometimes the choice of tenant is limited by the obligations of kinship. Yet tenants are interested in the quality of the land they will be working, and owners in the skill of prospective tenants. Both parties are able to judge, since the tenant knows the area and the landlord knows his neighbours. A tenant may be either a young man whom an older kinsman wants to help or a middle-aged one who is having difficulty in supporting all his children. Men of the latter type are definitely not uninterested in making the most of their share-cropped land. The landlord's share of the harvest is a matter of negotiation and depends on the productivity of the land; it may be fixed at various points between one and two thirds. Even where the parties are kin, the arrangements are formal and are insisted upon.

Malaysian official policy purports to protect the cultivator by recognizing only cash rents limited by law, and prohibits share-cropping. But in Kelantan the practice is still found so advantageous that the law cannot be applied. From the owner's point of view one reason for making such contracts is the high cost of wage labour. Their persistence has not prevented the adoption of many technical innovations.

There is more share-cropping in Kelantan than in any other part of Malaysia, and the reason must be a matter of local circumstances, as is the attitude of the Brazilian peasants described by Johnson. Clearly the tenant's lot may be very different in what we have come to regard as the typical Latin-American situation, where a mass of landless men can obtain subsistence on no other terms from landlords who can dictate their own conditions. Studies like the two cited here are not arguments for maintaining 'traditional' practices just because they are traditional. Rather they indicate that it is well to ask what kind of arrangement suits a given population before trying to force on them a stereotyped conception of 'modernisation'.

Fragmentation

The claim of every member of a right-holding group to a share of its land is made effective primarily through the division of any holding among the current holder's heirs, often during his lifetime, by assigning sections to his sons when they marry (to be cultivated by their wives). It follows logically that holdings must get smaller in every generation (assuming that population is continually increasing while available land does not increase, a condition that is usual at the present time). Moreover, sometimes individuals have inheritance rights in more than one piece of land, or in a village where they no longer live, so that holdings are not only fragmented but also dispersed. Thus, it has been assumed by both colonial and post-colonial re-formers, traditional inheritance rules have two kinds of ill effect; they reduce holdings below a viable size and they scatter them so that the farmer wastes his time walking between them.

The assumption that this, the apparently logical consequence, must inevitably result in practice has been held by many policy-makers, who can always point to instances that confirm it. But close observation shows that inheritance laws can be manipulated so that their operation need not have disastrous consequences. Arrangements by which outsiders can have the use of right-holders' land in a non-monetary economy have been described. Where commercial transactions in land are normal, there are questions to be asked. What *is* a viable holding? Objectively, it is one which would keep a family above a poverty line calculated on minimum acceptable standards of nutrition and health. For the farmer, however, it is what he regards as the least area that it is worth while to cultivate in terms of the income it will bring him, and this will vary in relation to ideas of the acceptable standard of living (ideas of the acceptable standard of nutrition may change too). The farmer in southern Italy can supplement what he owns by renting from another owner, perhaps an absentee, who may in this case be someone who has emigrated to America (Davis, 1973).

Where land is inherited in the male line, holdings may get smaller, but the land of an inheritance-group remains within a bounded area. It is when it can be transmitted by both men and women that a farmer can become possessed of holdings a long way apart. But he need not feel obliged to put up with the accidents of inheritance. Marriages between cousins are deliberately arranged to reunite both fragmented and dispersed holdings.

Land Reform Policies

But attempts to abolish traditional usages are only part of the wider policies that go by the name of 'land reform', and that aim in one way or another to free the peasants actually working the land from dependence on landlords who can demand whatever proportion they choose of the produce in sharecropping arrangements, or require people to give their labour in return for the holdings allotted to them. Many LDCs have nationalized their land, that is to say declared that all rights of ownership are vested in the state, but it is not always clear what practical consequences have followed. Chairman Mao's slogan 'The land to the tiller' precisely states the peasants' claim. Most of them would echo in one form or another the Russian *mouzhik*'s view that 'the land is God's and only those are entitled to hold it who work it with their own hands' (Jasny, 1949, p. 140).

Land reform is intended to raise the standard of living of peasants; that is what they expect of it, and as long as it does so they welcome it. Chairman Mao after the first stage of his reform – the dispossession of the 'rich peasants' – encouraged those who had received holdings to 'settle down and grow rich'. Even in Russia, Bukharin at the time of the New Economic Policy bade the peasants 'enrich themselves', but he was soon overruled in favour of a policy of compulsory deliveries at low prices. One of the given facts which land reform has to face is that peasants are, as was correctly perceived in Russia, inherently capitalistic. This fact has been confronted in different ways.

One way stops at making the peasant independent of a landlord or of any other directing authority. The other abolishes the exploiting landlord and replaces him by a bureaucratic authority which is by definition not exploitative.

Where it is assumed that the recipients of holdings will really be independent farmers, calculations have to be made of the amount of land available for distribution (which depends in part on the area to be fixed as the national or regional maximum), the area necessary to provide a family with what is regarded as an adequate income, and the size of farm considered to be most productive. Although many LDCs put their faith in large state-controlled farm units, some economists have calculated that small farms are more productive than large ones, though there is a minimum size – about three-quarters of an acre – below which this does not hold good.

Different countries vary greatly in the numbers to be provided for and in the amount of land that can be distributed. In Latin America there are vast areas of unused land and a rural population which, though crowded on the area open to it, is small in relation to them. In East and Central Africa much good land that had been alienated became available with independence and the departure of most of the expatriate owners, but the African populations of these countries are increasing very rapidly. It is in India and South-East Asia that the greatest difficulty has been found in meeting the needs of the landless and the peasants who have not enough land to make a living. An equal division of the land area in Java, for example, would leave the entire population without enough for subsistence.

It is only in the course of revolutions that landowners have been forcibly dispossessed. Where reforms are introduced by legislation and not by physical force, some kind of bargain has to be made. Compensation has to be offered, and this may be paid for out of general revenues or as a charge on the new owners. In the former case, they may still be paying it indirectly; in the latter it is just like a rent from their point of view. The size of maximum holdings must also be agreed on. Even then the potential losers have many means of evasion, especially where, as often happens, they have direct and indirect political influence; and the greater their wealth, the greater this will be. The example of India is most often cited. Every state in India enacted a land reform law soon after independence, but by 1970 only 0.3 per cent of the cultivated land had been reallocated, and that mostly of inferior quality.

Joint families who had managed a large area as a single enterprise could formally divide it among the members so that none had more land than the permitted minimum. It is even said that, when they had done so, the individual members would apply for the subventions offered to 'small farmers' (in Srinivasan and Bardhan, 1974). Of Latin America, it has been asserted that 'laws are approved with the tacit agreement that they will not be vigorously enforced' (Stavenhagen, 1970, p. 77).

The areas that landlords have been allowed to keep in different countries – or even in different regions depending on conditions of soil and climate – vary so widely that it is of little value to compare them. Lipton (1977) has suggested for Bangladesh the kind of strategy that would produce the best attainable results with the least friction. He is here writing of a densely populated country where there are not many estates that would generally be considered 'large'. He calculates that to take land from only the largest 5 per cent of owners would meet with much less opposition than to take it from the top 10 per cent, and would not yield much less for distribution; and that to cut the maximum holding from 10 to 7 acres would penalise – and anger – four times as many people and not even double the area of land released. He also raises the question whether the land acquired should go to the landless or be used to make up existing mini-farms to a viable size. The landless may be the more unfortunate, but each of them would need a larger share of the distributable land. 'To distribute non-viable shares to the landless', he writes, 'is a sentimental but ineffective method of improving their situation' (Lipton, 1977, p. 286) So, he argues, various compromises must be found, and above all, other means of livelihood should be created for the landless, for example employing them to look after irrigation works.

Attitudes towards land reform in the LDCs have been greatly influenced by the Soviet view that poor peasants were exploited by rich ones, a dogma that was taken over by Chairman Mao. In the first days of his victory he encouraged the 'middle' and 'poor' peasants – categories first set up in Russia – to attack the rich ones by force. Later they tended to be satisfied with a peaceful redistribution, among other reasons because they did not like quarrelling with their neighbours. 'Peaceful land reform', however, was officially disapproved because 'only the legitimacy that angry mass participation would provide' (Shue, 1980, p. 82) could finally establish the power of the people. But if middle and poor peasants 'settle down and grow rich', some at least of them will become rich peasants. And what then?

Collectivization

Then policy switches to collectivization, the mode of production that in any case conforms logically to socialist ideology, with the state farm as an auxiliary to it. On a state farm a worker is an employee, though he may be assigned a small area to cultivate on his own. In a co-operative he is a socialist man working with his fellows for the good of all, as was natural for mankind before – well, when? Where large agricultural enterprises have been nationalised, as in some Latin American countries, it has been thought necessary to keep them as units for the sake of maintaining production and keeping up exports.

The Chilean land reform, which was aborted by the overthrow of Allende, has had most publicity on account of its dramatic beginning and end. A sympathetic but critical observer (Steenland, 1977) has told the firsthand story of one of the collectives which were spontaneously formed under the guidance of a team of young *Miristas*, and lasted for three years. It had 25 members. Its officers were a president, treasurer and a foreman elected annually. The last-named assigned the day's tasks every morning. There were four tractor drivers, who could be demoted if they caused damage to the machinery. A cowherd and a night watchman were appointed for a month at a time, the latter to keep an eye on the cows. The rest shared the general work of fencing, building, weeding, harvesting and carrying loads. The president and treasurer did not really understand their financial situation, and since the collective was always in debt there was no bonus to be shared. 'Most peasants', says Steenland, 'understood that it was their duty to work collectively and sell their co-operative produce to the government so that it could in turn be sold to the workers in the city at low official prices ... They understood that increased production would help feed the workers in the cities.'

Still, they found it hard to learn how to run the farm as a group. They disregarded collective decisions and no one would put pressure on delinquents. Some used the communal tools and failed to return them. Someone rented out the communal thresher on his own account, others borrowed the communal tractor on Sundays for their private plots, and also diverted to them the communal provision of seed and fertiliser. In 1972 almost half a peasant's cash income came from outside the co-operative, either from his small permitted private area, from an equally small plot that he still owned in the Indian reservation, or from share-cropping.

A more sceptical account of the Chilean reform (Schuh, 1978) ascribes to the collective farming policy a steep decline in food production and rise in food imports in the two years when the official policy was in force, and also asserts that wage-labourers were better off than the collectivised farmers. But it is open to anyone to argue that it would have produced better results if it had had a longer time to work. Nevertheless, similar difficulties are reported from nearly all the newly created collectives. The usual solution, however, has not been to disband them but to make more determined efforts to explain to the members what their 'objective situation' is (and also to use force where this can be made effective).

But why, a naive enquirer might ask, don't peasants understand their objective situation? If it is their duty to sacrifice themselves for a community extending far beyond their ken, how is it that they have no sense of this until they have been re-educated? Towards whom *do* people have a sense of duty? First and foremost to their families and their immediate kin, then to those of their neighbours with whom they have relationships of reciprocity. In literate societies with wide-ranging means of communication, to more impersonal oganizations. Hardly ever to the furthest bounds of a political unit. And peasants do not live in literate societies with wide-ranging means of communication. So they are no readier to treat collective property with scrupulous care than the majority of dwellers in squatters' communes or than the wreckers of telephone kiosks. On the other hand, since they do have the entrepreneurship that they are so often supposed to lack, they do not scruple to turn such property to their own advantage when they can. Ultimately, the peasant attitude to possession of land depends on the fact that he can see what his labour produces as a worker in a mine or factory cannot, and he wants to decide what it is to produce as much as he wants to control the return that the product brings in.

Some case histories

The most recent examples of land reform are, unsurprisingly, in the countries which have most recently become independent. Thus, independent Botswana has introduced new land laws, not primarily to give security to cultivators but with the aim of increasing production by the more efficient use of resources, and also as a movement towards a democracy and national unity which the new rulers thought was obstructed by the recognition of chiefs over separate areas. All the 'tribal' land – that is the areas that were once designated 'native reserves' – was taken over by the government, and in each of the eight tribal areas a Land Board was made responsible for exercising the powers formerly held by chiefs. An election manifesto assured the voters that this would give them greater security than they had had when they were subject to the 'whims' and 'arbitrary decisions' of the chiefs (phraseology that could be paralleled from the statements of colonial authorities who thought parliamentary democracy was synonymous with civilization). In practice chiefs were appointed to Land Boards, though they formed a minority of the members. The Boards exercised their powers in accordance with the directives of the government, or what they took to be such. The government believed, as does President Nyerere of Tanzania, that progress called for the grouping of scattered homesteads into concentrated villages. In the case of Botswana it was assumed that this would reduce the cost of social services, and development grants were offered as an incentive to gather in villages. It was also assumed that the overgrazing which erodes the soil and destroys its fertility would be better controlled if grazing areas were marked out and one allotted to each village. The law provided that anyone who left his land uncultivated for five years 'without reasonable excuse' would lose his right to it, whereupon it could be allotted to someone more deserving. The reasonable and unanswerable excuse was that the poor soils of Botswana needed a much longer period of fallow, but some Boards made no exception to the five-year rule.

Since it is traditional for the Tswana to live in concentrated villages where water is available, the new policy affected them only where the Land Boards drew up and enforced zoning plans for residence, cultivation and grazing, and not many Land Boards have been able to do this. But the people of the Tati Reserve are not Tswana, but Kalanga. They had never been subject to a single chief, nor had they ever lived in villages. People had moved from one area to another as population pressed or soil became exhausted, making personal arrangements with kinsmen who had hereditary rights. Now such arrangements were called 'self-allocation' and were disapproved if not penalised; they did not confer any right that the authorities would recognise. The Kalanga thought it was the cancellation of their accustomed rights that was arbitrary; and they thought the new laws were another attempt by the Tswana majority to turn them into Tswana. The sub-chiefs, as the heads of the separate groups were officially called, were appointed to the Land Board, and as often happens when a previously limited authority is extended, they, with their fellow Board members, took what the population in general regarded as 'arbitrary decisions'. The worst such decision is to redistribute forfeited land among members of the allocating authority, and this has sometimes been done, though it has not been asserted that all Land Boards operate in this way, or that the central government does not try to control them.

This information comes from an anthropologist, Richard Werbner, and it would not have come, or not so soon, from a differently qualified investigator. Should we have offered remedies for the difficulties that he observed? Or offered to rewrite history so as to show what would have been a better policy? This is more than most anthropologists would expect to do. What they can do is to point up problems that policy-makers have not suspected. The people whose discontents they register are usually those who, rightly or wrongly, see no advantage for themselves in the new order, but it is not for them to say whether the authorities ought not to press on with the new order. They can, however, sometimes show where innovations have not had the results expected of them; for example, according to Werbner, it has not turned out to be cheaper to provide social services for nucleated villages than for the scattered homesteads in which many people were living before. They can show what it is that villagers who have not been consulted dislike or fail to understand; though they should also emphasise the importance of consultation and explanation with people whose lives are going to be affected. But it has to be left to governments to decide when to impose compulsion for the sake of a greater good, and when to conciliate the discontented for the sake of some compromise. Moreover, if a scheme fails of its objective, it is not enough to say that the people have not been consulted; it is necessary to understand, as an anthropologist should, obstacles that have their roots in situations that the people affected take for granted and do not analyse.

The most recent news of all comes from Zimbabwe, where, since independence, six areas of hitherto unused or under-utilised land have been bought from white farmers for allocation to Africans. The largest, at Gutu, south of Salisbury, covers 80,000 acres and comprises 33 former farms. Settlement here began late in 1980, and by April 1981, just a year from Independence Day, 528 farmers had each been allotted an acre for a house site and 12 acres for farming (much of it probably to be devoted to grazing), and a minimum of seeds, fertiliser and tools. Not all the allottees arrived in time to plant for this year's harvest 'due to some initial mix-ups' (bureaucratic tangles, inevitable in a brand-new administration?); the late-comers depend on an emergency food programme supposed to end in April 1981. Altogether 1,500 families had been settled on a total of 300,000 acres, not the best quality land, a reason why the owners had been willing to sell. In Zimbabwe the import-ance of efficient commercial farming is recognised, and there was at that time no question of compulsory purchase, let alone compulsory collectivization, though the Minister for Lands expressed the hope that farmers would come to see the value of co-operative production (*The Times*, 7 Apr 1981).

By a coincidence, one of the few studies of the attitudes of

African farmers towards settlement schemes to have been made by an anthropologist concerns earlier types of land settlement in Rhodesia (as it then was). Under Rhodesian administration, the bulk of the area allotted for African occupation was called Tribal Trust Land, and in it traditional land rights were observed, but there were specified Native Purchase Areas where farmers who attained a prescribed standard of efficiency could buy land. This became their individual property when they had completed the necessary payments; up to that time they could be evicted for bad farming. From about 1969, irrigation schemes were introduced in some parts of the Tribal Trust Land; there Africans could lease plots, paying for the water, and hold them as long as they followed the instructions of extension officers.

In the Purchase Areas the individual holdings were larger than the area that would have been available in the Tribal Trust Land. This was their advantage for the ambitious farmer. Another advantage perceived by many was that they were not under the control of chiefs whom they regarded as un-enlightened. But they arrived as individuals without any established links with their neighbours, and their homesteads were so far apart that it was not easy to make or keep up acquaintances. They could not replace the close-knit communities in which neighbours joined in working parties in the busy seasons; but in any case some people preferred to employ paid labour rather than be committed to reciprocal work on others' fields. Only one family of father, mother and children could live on one farm, a provision which has been retained in the new law throwing open the whole territory to African purchase; an African view of this restriction on the normal development of the extended family is that this simply stultifies the measure. The Purchase Area farmers tried to increase the size of their own families by marrying plural wives and keeping their unmarried or divorced children with them; this was their way of ensuring a stable and adequate labour force. But as only one son could inherit a farm, only the eldest was usually much interested in it, and the others preferred to look for work in a town. As for the girls, they knew they would not have to work so hard in the larger family groups of the Trust Lands, and, although they could expect to be in a poorer home there, that was where they hoped to find husbands. Their mothers encouraged them in this, while their fathers wanted them to marry neighbours.

On the irrigation schemes the plot-holders resented the close supervision, as indeed have many beneficiaries of land redistribution policies. A good many kept their Trust Land holdings, and some regarded the plots as a supplementary source of income, as they would regard wage labour. Others stayed only long enough to buy a holding in a purchase area. On this point a contrast may be drawn with Kenya, where irrigated holdings have been offered of an area calculated to produce an income high enough to make it worth while accepting the controls (Carruthers, 1976). This, naturally, is a source of inequality; the income potential, which irrigation is of course expected to increase, may be markedly higher than that on adjacent unirrigated land. In the most successful cases it is five times as great. But a proposal to aim at lower incomes and settle twice the number of families on plots half the size seems to have been found impracticable.

Land reform, then, has not succeeded in equalizing incomes, and is not likely to, though it may well enable many people to 'settle down and grow rich' even if such people do not start from the very bottom of the ladder. It seems perverse to grudge a benefit to people who are poor enough in all conscience because it has not gone instead to others who are poorer still.

Extension Services

But there is one form of inequality which does call for a remedy. That is in access to sources of information. Effective access to extension services is not in practice open to all. Extension workers encourage those farmers who see the point of their demonstrations and do not need much prodding to follow their advice. They are quite right. This is what most teachers do, though some are better than others at bringing on the backward. Those who are in most need of help are the slowest to understand and/or the poorest. Both these differences are important. But another difference, which ideally should be of no importance at all, usually is quite significant.

This is the distance of the farmer from the extension worker's base. Some people have further to go to ask for advice, or apply for selected seed or fertiliser, or anything else that they may be entitled to, and this may well debar them from even asking.

But where existing extension work is criticised, it is on the ground that advice at least should be offered and not have to be sought at some office. Of course it is the line of least resistance for an extension worker to concentrate his efforts on the more responsive individuals. It is easy to ascribe this preference to his lack of dedication. No doubt few extension workers have the zeal of missionaries, but they may well be as conscientious as other government servants. It is worth considering, as has Janice Jiggins (1977), some obstacles resulting from the present organization of extension work that no amount of dedication could overcome. Although her discussion is couched in general terms, it gives the impression of referring primarily to India, with its elaborate organization of Village Level Workers.

The obstacles are a matter of the recruitment and training of extension officers, the tasks set them and their relations with their superiors. Whereas the ideal extension officer would have an answer to all the villagers' doubts and difficulties, a ready ear to all their questions and the kind of personality that invites contact, the real-life one has been selected on rather narrow qualifications for a low grade in the bureaucratic hierarchy, and is paid less than he would be if he was employed by a commercial company. (In Nigeria the conditions of service and 'motivation' of employees of the Nigerian Ministry of Agriculture and the private enterprise Nigerian Tobacco Company were compared in similar terms some years earlier (Harrison, 1978).) He is liable to be transferred before he has had time to make effective contacts. His hopes of promotion are focused on transfer from the 'field' to a head office, not only because that would be an easier life, but because there is no promotion which would enable him to do the extension work with higher status and more responsibility. He must satisfy his superiors with evidence of work done, that is numbers of visits made, and of successes achieved, that is numbers of applications for new seeds or fertilisers. He can get most out of his usually inadequate transport by visiting places near roads, and will be most readily listened to by those farmers who have already begun to make innovations. His superiors are more concerned to see that he is earning his pay than to help him to solve problems the nature of which they do not know much about. To meet their requirements he has to spend – in making out reports – time that could be given to discussion with villagers.

His job is not in fact to deal with practical difficulties. It is to sell a package of recommended improvements, some perhaps farming methods, some physical inputs such as fertiliser or high-yielding seeds. It is by the number who apply for the package that his efficiency is judged. Its contents may be changed at any time by higher authority, but although this might be an excellent thing if it led to the devising of a range of packages suitable to different circumstances, such as will always be found within a single administrative district, in fact the changes are more often dictated by some extraneous consideration such as shortage of a particular item. The extension officer is not consulted about what his area needs or wants. The traditional village suspicion of emissaries of government must be compounded when he seems to be merely uttering a string of stereotyped exhortations.

One remedy suggested by Jiggins would be to think of the extension officer not as a source of final authoritative information, but as a contact between the villager and specialists of various kinds – analogous to the Chinese 'barefoot doctors'.

In addition, an extension worker may be subject to pressure from men of importance who not only think it is their privilege to be first served, but can make his work difficult if he displeases them (again, not his fault). This kind of 'unfair competition' is most likely to be found in the lands of ancient civilization where societies have been stratified for many centuries; India is again the most conspicuous example. People of high caste will be listened to before people of lower castes, and they will be able to put in a word for their dependents too. In a slightly different field, that of co-operative societies, the report of a Rural Credit Survey organised by the Reserve Bank of India describes this situation:

The bigger landlord has ways which conform with those of

the moneylenders and indeed is often the moneylender or trader himself. The village headman is often drawn from the same class, and it is usual for them to have connections which link them not only to the sources of finance but to the seats of administrative powers. Subordinate officials, revenue and others – including many of the relatively low-paid co-operative department – have no alternative but to stay with these village leaders and be dependent on them for ordinary amenities when they visit the village . . . This close conformity of association and interests between the subordinate officials of government and the more powerful elements in the village is . . . of great significance in explaining the failure of implementation of . . . policies . . . emanating from the higher levels of administration.

These subordinate officials create for the benefit of their superiors . . . 'what might be called the illusion of implementation woven round the reality of non-compliance. Several factors in the village help to create this effect, not least among them the powerful influence of caste. If the leader is of a particular caste, it is unusual for others of the caste in the village to report to superior authority that things are otherwise than as reported by the village leader and the subordinate officials . . . The *status quo* and the non-compliance are achieved conjointly . . . by leading elements in the village and the subordinate agencies of government . . . The persons who suffer in this process are the weaker and disadvantaged elements of the village for whose benefit the directives and policies are conceived.' (All-India Rural Credit Survey, 1954, pp. 277–8)

Finally, a word should be said on the subject of language. In most LDCs a great number of different languages are spoken, and from these a few are selected for official communications. The speakers of this language are better placed than others, not only to understand the advice given them by extension agents, but also to ask for explanations and further information, or even, if they have the courage, to argue about the advantages of the new techniques that they are asked to adopt. Really effective extension officers would be able to talk in their own language with all villagers whom they visit; for this to be general it would be necessary for them to spend much more time in close contact with village life, and probably to be responsible for much smaller areas. In sum, a much higher proportion of resources ought to be devoted both to the training and remuneration of extension agents.

5

Women in Rural Life

Plans for agricultural development are apt to take for granted
that this is entirely a matter for men. It is men who own land
and among whom land is distributed in agrarian reforms; it is
men who raise loans to pay for fertilisers and other improvements. Often, though not always, it is they who dispose of the
family's cash income. So it is assumed that it is also men who do
the actual work in the fields, and men to whom extension
propaganda should be directed. Little attention is given to the
effect on women's work load of the adoption of the new
methods that are recommended. Nor has it been common –
though it is not entirely unknown – for small advances in
technology to be devised with the aim of lightening this load.
Another question that is not always asked, when men are urged
to adopt new methods which will need harder work but bring in
better returns, is: Who will do the work and who will get the
returns?

Another reason for the assumption that women are occupied
only in cooking and caring for children is that during the
colonial period this was the ideal that Europeans brought with
them, and that particularly through the education given by
missionaries, they tried to inculcate. They were not unaware
that women worked in the fields, sometimes more than men,
and they disapproved of men who 'made their wives work'.
Implicit in this attitude was another assumption: that the
question was not *what kind* of work men and women did, but
how much? Let men work harder and women would not have to
work so hard, the argument ran. Quite recently, the author of
an otherwise very perceptive study of the reasons why the
labour put into agriculture in Africa is very much less than it
might be, referring to The Gambia, where men work on
groundnuts and women on rice, spoke of 'the greater effort in
agriculture that could have been made had men and women
worked together' (Cleave, 1974, p. 112).

But anthropologists have shown that not only is there everywhere a recognized division of labour between men, women and children, but that such a division – as all over the world – is also a matter of status. Men are diminished by doing 'women's work', adults by doing 'children's work'. Boundaries are often broken down by the force of circumstance, but they do not fall like the walls of Jericho to exhortation alone.

Women's Work in the Family and Household

The basic questions that an anthropologist would ask would start with the village woman's daily work. When does her day begin and end? Must she walk long distances, carry heavy weights, manage cumbrous implements? If, for example, she makes pots, does she control the money that they bring in? What is the division of labour and of the reward where, as in West Africa, many women are petty traders and some trade on a considerable scale? Today women concerned with the status of their own sex, in the LDCs as well as in the rich countries, assert the right of women to be employed outside the home, and protest against their confinement to it. But losses and gains need to be balanced by examining the actual circumstances in which women work for wages.

In Muslim and Hindu societies men, and perhaps their wives too, are proud if they can demonstrate a high enough standard of living to be able to keep their women in seclusion, away from contact with males other than their brothers or husbands. Europeans living among such societies have generally seen little of village life, and in the cities have, until quite recently, had close contact mainly with the well-to-do who can attain the ideal of female seclusion; hence the widely accepted assumption that it is universal. Women living in seclusion do in fact make their own contribution to the productive process; but since they are in the minority it is better to consider first the share that women take in outdoor work in different LDCs.

Even at quite a low standard of living, women's work is sometimes lightened by assigning the hardest tasks to men who are not family members. But if there is no such outside labour, women are the 'hewers of wood and drawers of water'. They must go to rivers, wells or springs and carry home the household water on their heads in clay or brass pots, or nowadays kerosene tins, and they may have to go long distances. Some women of the Shilluk people who live along the west bank of the Nile are reported to walk five miles to the river for water, starting before dawn (White *et al.*, 1972, p. 107). This is admitted to be exceptional, but in a survey made in Tanzania, as many as one-third of the women in nine villages walked between one and two miles (ibid). Firewood is collected from the bush beyond the village fields. This too may call for long journeys, which get longer as population increases and cash crops extend cultivation areas, and it always involves carrying heavy loads. One account from India mentions branches six feet long. When there is no more bush within possible reach and dung is used for fuel, perhpas the task is easier.

Not many close studies of women's daily occupations have been made. One reason is that many anthropologists have been legitimately concerned with jural and political, as well as ritual, matters from which women were often excluded; another that few societies welcome the close attention of a strange man to women's affairs, and the majority of anthropologists are men. Such studies as there are have nearly all been made by women; and up to now women as well as men have tended to be more interested in public than in domestic matters. A new concern with the latter has appeared in recent years, but we have hardly begun to see its fruits, and some of the work done has been rather superficial.

One of the most detailed of recent accounts, not actually made by an anthropologist, is Hobson's (1978) of an Indian joint family in Bangalore, one of the poorest regions of India, in whose house she lived for some three months. This was regarded as the leading joint family in a village of 183 persons, and was the only one to employ a servant all the year round; he worked in the fields, mainly keeping irrigation channels open.

The women's day started at four in the morning with two hours grinding millet for the day's food, swinging round a heavy stone which pivoted on a stick. Then they prepared the first meal. The cattle dung was cleared out (the cattle sleep in the house), to be later carried to the fields. Water had to be fetched, firewood chopped, children dressed, dishes washed, sleeping blankets folded away, the house and its steps swept. Rice was husked in spare moments, by pounding it with a pole in a cavity in the floor. One women stayed at home to cook, the rest went to the fields, some leading animals with them, some with a basket on their heads full of manure, or else clothes to be washed. The outdoor work consisted in planting seeds, weeding, clearing stones from fields before they were ploughed, spreading manure. One woman had helped her son to dig a fifteen-foot well. Food was carried to the fields, for the men and for themselves. In the busy seasons when outside labourers were employed, the women brought the mid-day meal that was their payment. The pause for food was the one time for relaxation in the day. In the evening a meal was served for the men, and when at eleven they went to bed, the women woke the children to feed them, and then at last ate themselves.

There are few other equally detailed descriptive accounts, but several time-studies give an idea of the hours given to work of different kinds. Such a study in a village in The Gambia led to the conclusion that the average farming day, including the time spent walking to and from the field, was 5.7 hours for men and 6.8 hours for women; the women's day was longer because they had further to walk to the rice fields, for which they were responsible. They also worked on the farms a total of 159 days in the year compared with 103 for men. A number of other studies put the additional time spent on work in the house at somewhere between two and three hours. According to one calculation (Cleave, 1971), if time spent fetching wood and water is included, African women spend an additional four hours a day over and above their farm work. Even secluded women, in India and Africa, contribute to the production of food by winnowing or threshing the grain that their men harvest, and as the men take to growing high yielding varieties for sale, the amount of this work increases.

In parts of Africa, notably among the South-eastern Bantu, the religious significance of cattle debars women from contact with them, though among the Nuer only women may milk cows, and men's dependence on them for this essential activity enhances their status. In South Africa, where ploughing is now universal, women whose husbands are away at employment centres must hire a ploughman unless they have a kinsman at home – but if he undertakes the work, he will not expect to do it until he has ploughed his own fields, and the best of the season may be missed. The adoption of the plough, again, has made it possible to plant wider areas (provided there is enough land), and this again increases the woman's load in the subsequent operations. Some of the Gwembe Tonga who were re-settled when the Kariba Dam was built (see Chapter 8), had previously lived in tsetse country where they could not keep cattle. In their new homes they could plough with cattle – both beasts and ploughs often bought by men with the lion's share of the grant made in compensation for the move – and women found that there was much more work to do in their husbands' fields, sometimes so that they had to neglect land which belonged to them in this matrilineal society.

For Mapuche Indians in Chile (Steenland, 1977) there is another task that is familiar in the rich countries too, namely shopping. The women of Elicura Farm got the cash they needed in their largely monetized economy by selling chickens and vegetables which they brought with them to town; many were also carrying small children. They had to join queues of shoppers, in which of course the town dwellers were always ahead of them, and when they had bought, if they could, they had to wait till dusk for the only bus that would take them home. Steenland adds that women's other chores 'ranged from making blueberry pie to butchering pigs'. He further adds that these tasks 'were necessary to support the men and the reproduction of labour power' (p. 126).

Farm work depends on the seasons; there are peaks and slack times. But, as my generation grew up to learn, 'women's work is never done'; busy farming times for women mean not *some* work but *more* work. All through the year they are preparing and cooking the family's food and caring for the children. In a poor household which cannot afford to hire labour (and this is likely to be a monogamous household) the wife must step up her output of work at busy times or neglect her tasks in the home, or both. One of the busiest times is the planting season, when the farmer must make the most of what may be a short period of rain. In what geographers call the dry tropics, this follows a long dry period during which stocks of food run short, sooner or later according to the quantity that each household has been able to store from the previous harvest. Hunger reduces energy and increases vulnerability to disease, and it is just when hard work begins to be called for that disease is at its peak. Also, for reasons not altogether clear, births are most frequent at this time of year. So are deaths of newborn children. Mothers' milk is inadequate; they suckle their children less often and wean them earlier. But they must go on working, and all the harder in the poorer households where there are fewer people to share the work. Moreover, the distribution of available food is often unfavourable to women and children. Nearly everywhere men eat by themselves first and women and children take what is left. Among many African peoples certain foodstuffs are forbidden to women on various ritual grounds. Thus Ganda women may not eat mutton, and it is very common for women not to be allowed to eat eggs. This is definitely not a context where an anthropologist would say that local values must be respected, but he, and even she, would warn of the likely resistance to be met with in nutrition propaganda.

Women's Incomes

It is readily assumed that to raise the standard of living of a family it is sufficient to increase the household income. But this depends on the way in which income is distributed. It cannot be taken for granted that the cash earned by the head of a household will be used for the benefit of all its members, as indeed it could not be in Europe. Eleanor Rathbone, that pioneer of family allowances in Britain, urged that they should be paid direct to the mother on the ground that additional money received by the father would be spent on 'drinking and charabancing'; and if this is a puritanical judgment, the principle is sound enough.

But if one is asking what in fact does become of the higher incomes earned by increased production, it is important to know in any particular case what are the accepted principles of distribution within the family. Women may have sources of income under their own control. A woman may have a plot of land allotted to her with the right to dispose of the crop; or there may be some crops which are grown only by women; or, in countries with good communications and a fairly diversified economy, they may engage in petty or not-so-petty trade, sometimes travelling long distances.

A Tale woman in northern Ghana, at a time when deliberately promoted development had not touched that region, would be allotted a plot of ground by her husband for vegetables (additional work, of course) and could dispose of any that were surplus to her family's needs. She also had her own groundnut plot. If her kinswomen brought her presents of grain, they did not have to be merged in the household store. She could barter or sell her surplus, and thus buy pots and pans which became her property and passed to her daughters or sisters. She could sell or barter any pots or mats that she made (Fortes, 1949). In many LDCs women have long engaged in trade on their own account; they may be initially financed by their husbands, but once launched they usually operate independently.

Where the seclusion of women is a source of prestige, they may conduct operations from their own homes. Polly Hill (1969) has described the 'house-trade' of secluded Hausa women in the village of Batagarawa, six miles from Katsina in Nigeria. As she observed it, this trade fulfilled the function of a market-place for the exchange of surpluses within the village, as well as the sale of some goods from outside; attempts to establish a public market of conventional type repeatedly failed, since nobody wanted to deal there.

The women of Batagarawa, she says, 'sit, or work, in their courtyards all day . . . There they process foodstuffs, cook, trade and mind their children' (p. 394). In this case they may be trading on behalf of their husbands. The village is not self-sufficient in grain; much of what is grown is sold directly after the harvest, when urgent payments have to be made, and later in the year the sellers must buy what they need to eat. To meet this need some men buy grain outside the village and retail it through their wives; they decide what price is to be asked, though they cannot be sure that their orders will be obeyed.

More important, however, are women's independent activities. These consist mainly in the sale of foodstuffs – cakes and snacks, porridge, roasted groundnuts or groundnut oil, which they sell to children, to women who are bad at organizing their own cooking, to anyone who is hungry at midday, to young men who would rather eat out of doors than go home for their evening meal. They also sell vegetables, cosmetics and sometimes a range of shop goods. A successful woman trader may be much better off then her husband.

The women of Nupe in Nigeria, in an economy already highly monetized when Nadel described it in 1942, make a striking contrast to their sisters in India. They do not work in the fields at all, apart from occasional help at harvest time. They do collect the oil-palm fruits for which the men climb the trees, and they make the palm-oil and shea butter. Shea-nuts are women's exclusive property. But whereas the men of a family are wholly responsible for the production of the staple foodstuffs, certain indispensable ingredients of cooking have to be provided by women, who buy them in the market. They must, then, have some independent source of cash income. This may actually be the commission which a man pays his wife on the price for which she sells his surplus grain for him, or she may sell shea-nuts, or practise some craft such as pottery, weaving or dyeing, though by no means all women are craft workers. Women make titbits to sell, and if their own husbands want to eat them, they have to pay.

But over and above this, many women make a profession of trading, and go long distances by canoe or train, leaving their homes for considerable periods of time, sometimes even years. A farmer's wife, who is expected to look after his house, cannot do this; it is an occupation for the wives of the better-off, who can employ servants. Such women, in the nature of things, are entirely independent, and in the more distant past it was considered permissible only for childless women or those who were too old for childbearing to engage in long-distance trade. But as trade and communications developed under British administration, more and more women, including young ones with children, came to adopt this mode of life. Buchi Emecheta's novel, *The Slave Girl* (1977), gives a picture of the Ibo women who retail imported cloth in the Onitsha market.

Scarlett Epstein's (1962) comparison of the two South Indian villages, Wangala which received irrigation and Dalena which was bypassed by the canal, shows how the position of women was differently affected in the two cases. In Wangala, the men who did well out of cash cropping kept their women at home, though not in seclusion, and boasted that their daughters knew nothing about farm work. Women had always been responsible for the care of buffaloes, and allowed to keep the money they earned by selling milk. Now that they are free from farm work they can concentrate on this; they go to the neighbouring town to sell their butter and buy anything they want, and they lend money, in small amounts but for high interest. In Dalena, where men either buy irrigated land in other villages or pursue the new economic opportunities that irrigation has brought to the region as a whole, they leave their wives in complete charge of the home farms where food is grown; without the women's work they could not seek profit outside. The one advantage that the new times brought to Dalena women was the installation of a flour mill by one of the village entrepreneurs. This saved them many hours of pounding and winnowing, and one or two of them took to keeping buffaloes and selling milk. But most of them simply gave more time to looking after house and children, or even to leisure; and who can blame them?

Although it is unusual for women to work for wages in the rural areas of LDCs, this does sometimes happen. Two examples may be given from rice cultivation, one from South India, one from Africa. In both these regions (and doubtless elsewhere) the transplantation of rice is women's work. In Epstein's villages the Untouchable women form teams of ten or twelve for this purpose. They are paid in rice, not by the day but by the area covered; they work on different landowners' fields in turn. If they were asked to adopt the slower but more productive Chinese and Japanese methods of transplanting, they would have to work longer for the same reward, which has been fixed by long custom and which the village council is not willing to change. Hence only those farmers who have bought land outside their own village and can employ daily (male) wage labour there can follow the new methods recommended to them.

In The Gambia, rice cultivation was, until very recently, regarded as entirely women's work. Women who had rice fields of their own organised groups among themselves to work on different fields in turn at the busy seasons. In 1966 the irrigation of swamp lands was introduced with the advice of a Taiwanese agricultural mission, and plots were leased to men, who adopted the Chinese method. Women still do all the transplanting and weeding, in which they are very skilled. But very few households include enough women to do this without additional help, and this is obtained by offering wages to women who are under no obligation to work for the plot-holder.

Who Receives Cash Income and How is it Allocated?

The assumption that an African or Asian husband, because he is the head of his family, disposes of all its members' earnings, has been shown to be false by the instances cited. But it is still made, and it can have unhappy practical consequences. An illustration may be drawn from the failure of a co-operative society that was set up for the marketing of pyrethrum in Kenya. This was formerly a plantation crop for which the labour was supplied by women and children, whose small fingers were better suited than men's to the delicate operation of plucking the flowers. Independent Kenya adopted the policy of substituting co-operative marketing from individual holdings for wage labour. The plot-holders were men, and so, accordingly, were the co-operative members. So, though the women were still expected to do most of the work, when the crop was sold the proceeds went to the men, and the women no longer got what they had had before from their employers. The co-operative did not last (Apthorpe,1969).

There are, in fact, very few societies in which the normal household is not headed by a man, who is expected to provide for his dependents even if this means no more than organizing the production of food and distributing the product. But with the development of cash cropping, to which all today's projects are directed, new questions arise about the distribution of the money earned. In most cases the payment is practically, if not theoretically, at the free disposal of the person who sells the crop; it is paid to him (or her) and nobody can stop him (or her) from spending part or all of it at once. But there are certain established norms regarding the obligations of a husband or father. As imported goods become available, the level of what are considered to be basic necessities is constantly rising, low though it may still be by the standards of the rich countries. In Central Africa men are expected to provide their wives with clothes; failure to do so is a ground for divorce. But *how many* clothes? 'He does not clothe me' usually means 'He is away in the city and sends me nothing.' Where the husband is at home, earning money by the sale of a crop, the question how much of this should go to his family may be more complicated.

It is one which development policies cannot directly take into account, and indeed the complaints of women who do earn incomes that are under their own control can well be seen as the discontents of people whose situation is improving, but not as quickly as they would wish. Development agents can do no more than ask whether a fair share of the rewards for the adoption of new practices goes to those who actually do the extra work.

However, in one instance at least, although women have no independent source of income, they have considerable control over the family resources. This is in southern Java, where Jay (1969) found that from the moment of establishing a separate household (which he calls a 'hearth-hold') a wife is in 'undisputed control over daily expenditure'. Husbands did not even check on what was spent, and had to ask their wives for money for their own purchases. Women made the day-to-day decisions about the food supply, about selling crops and buying clothing and household goods, about paying wages (when they could afford to employ labour) and about expenditure on feasts and rituals. There were decisions (evidently about daily housekeeping) 'into which the husband is not even permitted to enquire' (Jay, 1969, p. 92). But there do not seem to be many comparable cases.

It is clear then that in such matters there may be great differences in different societies, and such differences must surely be relevant also to the attitude of women towards the additional work that technical improvements may involve.

Moreover, it is not only in the rich countries that women are demanding a greater say in decisions that affect them, and sometimes even forming associations for economic activity. One example is the Self-employed Women's Association, which is sponsored in Gujarat by the textile workers' union originally founded by Gandhi. The leaders of this organisation, which has been in existence only since 1975, have been active in expressing the general problems of villagers, men as well as women, and in collecting data to support their arguments. This work is evidently prompted by an educated minority. An anthropologist would be interested in the question whether the social structure of these villages was particularly propitious for the assertion of women's claims to be heard, and if so, in what respects it differed from that found elsewhere in India.

An item which appeared in *The Economist* (18 Aug 1979) describes the women's clubs that have been, or are to be, set up in every village in Indonesia. Some of them have asserted feminine equality by forming gamelan orchestras, an activity previously confined to men, and they play their instruments to summon the club members to their weekly meetings. The account of these clubs' achievements seems too good to be true. Where there is a club, infant mortality goes down and family planning up, there are more village crafts, better fish ponds, better fruit trees, better gardens, more poultry . . . Even if the correspondent only saw a few of the 20,000 villages with women's clubs, they illustrate a line of advance with potentialities. Whereas men, the article says, see village improvement in terms of stereotypes – irrigation, electrification – women concentrate on immediate small-scale needs such as vitamin pills, a scale to weigh babies, a typewriter. Javanese officials on tour, the report states, take their wives with them to talk to the village women. Foreign advisers do not; and if they did, would their wives just regard the trip as a holiday tour? There is a lesson here.

But to be of the same sex as your audience is by itself no more a recipe for success than to be of the same country. Knowledge of other ways of life than your own is still important. A less happy story of Indonesia is that of some members of the left-wing nationwide women's movement which was active shortly before the country became independent. They were the wives of better-off villagers, who gained prestige from their membership of this sophisticated, urban-based, association. In one village they launched a campaign against the 'wasteful' traditional practice whereby, once a year, every household sent a tray of cooked food to all its neighbours. This, they rightly said, laid a heavy burden on the poorer households. They pursued the campaign by putting it about that the national movement had 'ordered' the exchange to be limited to the close kin of each house, and they succeeded in making the change. But the poorer women were not pleased. They had enjoyed the sense of community on the day when rich and poor exchanged as equals in status – and at the same time the poor got better presents than they gave. The restriction was effective for a year or two; it is not known whether it lasted. This example shows that it is not enough to be a member of the community you want to improve; it is still necessary to understand what people's values are. It recalls the efforts of well-meaning British officials in India to set up 'Better Living Societies' the members of which would agree to cut down their expenditure on weddings.

In contrast with this story is one that seems more of a piece with the activities of the women's clubs. In 1975, in six villages in western Java, eight or ten mothers were chosen from each and given a short training in the cooking and demonstration of balanced meals – making them in effect into extension workers. These women persuaded the mothers of undernourished children to form groups who would attend a series of demonstrations for three months, and give the children the food recommended. The mothers were impressed by the marked improvement in their children's health. The main new ingredients were locally available green vegetables. Anthropologists would take care to avoid recommending additions to diet (even such apparently simple ones as eggs) which village mothers would not take up because they could sell them to buy more of the staple foodstuff, rice.

It is surely obvious that the instruction disseminated by extension workers in agriculture is most successful when it reaches directly the people who will actually be working on the land. Here the difficulty that most extension workers come from the cities, and may themselves have no practical experience of agriculture, is compounded by the fact that most of them are men. Where women are not expected to have any contact with men who are not related to them, this channel of communication is not open. And in any case, the instruction given is usually concentrated on cash crop cultivation.

In fact, the segregation of the sexes is too often carried over into the development organization. Agriculture is regarded as a matter for men, on which men instruct men. Women are approached by women on subjects held to be the concern of women – child care, nutrition, hygiene. Indeed these do concern women, and in some societies men are not much interested in them. The mistake is to suppose that agriculture does not concern women. If women were trained as agricultural extension workers – separately from men if this was thought necessary – they might well be better placed to know what improvements were practicable and desirable. A happy exception to these generalisations, however, has been described in the Farmers' Training Centres in Kenya, where short courses of one or two weeks were given to men and women together (the report is of 1963). Two-thirds of those attending were men, one-third women. The women were also taught some 'home economics', which made their presence in the courses 'more acceptable' to the men (De Wilde, 1967, p. 191). Such a consideration angers feminists, but one may ask two questions: Did the women like this instruction? and Did it negate the value of the farming instruction?

As for the 'women's' subjects, a conference of women interested in development planning which was held in 1977 made the point that the different 'welfare' extension services should be presented in a single package *along with agriculture.* All the 'welfare' services are intended to raise standards of living, as is the newest one, family planning. Improvements in health and nutrition, while on the one hand they should indirectly increase productivity, also often call for the allocation of family resources to new ends, and so impose on the household an immediate need to increase its productive resources. The education of children requires their parents to forego their productive labour. Better child care is likely at the least to need more time. Hence these various forms of improvement should not be offered separately to two different *publics*, one of men, one of women. But in countries where they do have to be offered to segregated *audiences*, both men and women must be trained as communicators. It has also been remarked that it would do no harm for men to hear the instruction on nutrition and child care.

One question that anthropologists might pursue is the way in which ideas circulate in any given community. In Kenya, for example, it was found that new notions about farming are spread in encounters between women in the village or at the market. The importance of identifying informal communication networks of this kind and perhaps associating them with more formal organisations was suggested at the conference just mentioned.

Whether development schemes are directed to the alleviation of poverty in general or to women's circumstances in particular, it is clear that where agriculture is concerned, appropriate improvements cannot be devised without detailed knowledge of existing methods. For women especially, the question how much time their work takes up is most directly relevant to the possibility of gathering them together for instruction. At the very simplest, an extension programme should take account of busy and slack seasons and even times of day. But it is also important to know how the time is distributed between the various tasks, and also just in what way the tasks are done.

The object of such knowledge is not only to relieve women of heavy physical labour, but to enable them to have time even to listen to information about possible improvements, let alone adopt them. This could bear on the question how far women could be expected to walk to an extension centre, and hence on the distribution of such centres. Such data would also indicate where there was most need for labour-saving devices and what form these devices would most appropriately take.

6
Equality

The authors of the American Declaration of Independence wrote 'We hold this truth to be self-evident, that all men are created equal.' The next historic revolution, the French, had as its watchword 'Liberty, Equality, Fraternity'. Both phrases applied in the beginning to equality of political rights, and both were at first associated with the right to possess property and use it to the best advantage. Later revolutionaries, holding that that kind of liberty can only lead to exploitation, see that liberty and equality cannot both be maximized at the same time, and plump for equality. As a distinguished contemporary philosopher (Kolakowski, 1978, p. 186) puts it:

> Taken to an extreme, this means that it matters less whether people have much or little so long as they all have the same. If there is a choice between improving the lot of the poor but allowing inequality to subsist, or leaving the poor as they are, and depressing everyone to their level, it is the second alternative that must be chosen.

Not many policy makers today, perhaps none at all, would accept this principle in so stark a form, although, as has been sufficiently indicated already, most of them see it as one of the aims of development to narrow the gap between rich and poor. But some do try to organize development in such a way that nobody gets ahead of his neighbours, and in Africa it is argued, notably by President Nyerere, that this kind of equality was part of an African tradition that only needs to be revived now that colonial rule is ended.

But it is hardly possible to stimulate development without creating inequalities, and though strategies exist for mitigating them, if too much emphasis is laid on preventing their appearance, development policies may be stultified altogether.

The very process of development creates inequalities. It may lead to the abolition of traditional privileges; it does give new opportunities to people who in its absence could expect no better material standards than their parents had. But it has never created a situation in which the beneficiaries advanced shoulder to shoulder on a broad front at an equal pace. Indeed it may well be that only in conditions of extreme shortage are really egalitarian societies to be found. It does not take much imagination to see the reason why, but what it does need is an ability to picture in the mind's eye real events actually happening. The resources available for development are not unlimited, and would not be even if aid givers were more generous than in fact they are. The number of people who know how to organize development projects is limited too. They need specific knowledge which is not so easily acquired. Development cannot be sprayed all over a country by helicopter. It has to begin *somewhere* in the literal sense of that word.

How choose the place? It must be accessible; it had better have climatic and soil conditions in which new crop varieties can flourish and the extra labour demanded by new techniques does not risk being wasted. Hence it is likely to be already better-off than other parts of the same country.

The shortage of skilled development workers in the LDCs has been mentioned in an earlier chapter. Those who have the necessary skills have gained them by a long process of study, and they consider that they deserve the rewards that this entitles them to; exhortations to moderate their claims are seldom effective, and this is an additional reason for differences in living standards between town and country. Those at the highest level – perhaps 'professionals' rather than skilled workers – can emigrate to places, among them the various agencies of the United Nations, where rewards are higher, as indeed unskilled workers from East Africa do to the oil-rich countries. China under Chairman Hua admits the need for incentive payments as Russia did long ago. True, differences are now related to the contribution made to production and not to the control of productive capital, but it is no good pretending that there are no differences.

In agriculture, differences of individual aptitude may be more important just because farmers are not thought to require any speical skill. Some are cleverer than others, quicker to see the advantages of new techniques presented to them, perhaps even to invent some for themselves. Some are readier to take risks, and this may well be because they are already better off and so less afraid of failure. No 'free' government interested in increasing food production is going to stop them for the sake of equality.

In Asia with its age-old stratification, the advocates, such as they are, of the reduction of inequality see it as a move towards a better form of society. In Africa it has been constantly asserted, especially in the early days of independence, that social classes only began to appear in a traditionally 'classless' society when it was subjected to colonial rule. Julius Nyerere has been mentioned. 'We in Africa', he has said, 'have no more need of being "converted" to socialism than we have of being "taught" democracy . . . Modern African socialism can draw from its traditional heritage the recognition of "society" as an extension of the basic family unit' (Nyerere, 1962). Very similar ideas were held of the (actually widely different) societies of West Africa by the young French Marxists who took teaching posts in the colonies at the time of Leon Blum's Popular Front in 1936. They did not command the agreement of all African nationalists, some of whom thought the power of hereditary chiefs, of which they were well aware, was an existing abuse which had been compounded when European authorities recognized them.

The thesis that I am arguing here is that there has never been a completely egalitarian society, let alone one based on undiscriminating co-operation, and that the nature of social stratification in different societies, and the current attitudes towards it, are matters that should be known to anyone concerned with development.

Possible Bases of Inequality

No society at all can get on without some means of organizing such co-operative activities as it pursues. Nyerere admits the existence of 'elders', the senior men of descent groups. But for some purposes leadership must extend beyond a group within which it rests ultimately on the sentiment of kinship; in the societies which have very little political co-ordination such purposes may be the launching of a raid or war, or the making of an alliance for the prosecution of feuds. The leader in such societies does not have a permanent position, a recognized office; he is looked up to for his personal qualities, *but also*, usually, because he has that small surplus of wealth, where everyone has very little, that enables him to do favours and put others under an obligation to him. Such leaders have some-times been able to consolidate their position, even make it hereditary, under colonial rule. If they retain it still, it is because they belong to populations such as the Bedouin Arabs, whose habitat is so difficult that no serious effort has been made to develop it (what has been done in Libya is to expend the proceeds from the export of oil in creating cities at the oases, where many former nomads now live while controlling lorry-borne desert trade).

More significant are the societies which have long recognized a distinction – what Nyerere would call an opposition when he is denying its existence – between rulers and ruled. The rulers have been called chiefs in most of Africa, Emirs in the Muslim-ruled areas, in British parlance never kings, since there could be only one king in territory counted as British. Haile Selassie in Ethiopia was even an emperor.

There has never been a formal classification of chiefs of different degrees of importance. Those whom all would agree to call petty had authority over small culturally homogeneous populations. But conquests began early, and every state of any size had its subject peoples. The sharpest division was that found in the kingdoms of western Uganda, Rwanda, and Burundi, where an aristocracy of pastoral invaders ruled a lower class of longer-established agriculturalists. Nearly every-where there were war captives, not always, but often, called slaves. They did not form a permanent class, since they generally married into their masters' families, and after that it was thought right to forget their alien origin; but it was cast up against them in quarrels, and it debarred them from the highest political offices. The overseas slave trade stimulated the demand for slaves, but did not create it.

In the great trading states of West Africa, hereditary rulers organized their kingdoms through numbers of titled subordinates, a small but highly placed number of whom were slaves. In general they maintained their authority over con-quered neighbours by recognizing their rulers as vassals, who retained their internal power as long as they met their overlords' demands for tribute and military service. European rule differed from that of earlier invaders in that it went much further in changing, deliberately as well as inadvertently, the social norms of its new subjects. But it too began by maintain-ing an established élite in power.

Where, and in so far as, the recruitment of élites has come to have a different source, this has been one of the consequences of changes in the distribution of wealth. The new élites are those who made the most of new economic opportunities while the traditional ruling classes trusted to the security of their revenues. In those African societies where there was no tradition of literacy, education in the language of the colonial rulers was not only an asset in business but an entry into professions requiring European qualifications, notably the law and, later, medicine. It also made the students familiar with the ideology of democracy, which they could turn against their rulers, although they later came to interpret it in very different ways themselves. Education was not free, but it did not necessarily depend on parental income; a boy could earn his own school fees by doing odd jobs or take time out to work in the middle of a university course, as many still do. Obafemi Awolowo, who became the first Premier of Western Nigeria, and is now (1983) one of his country's elder statesmen, paid for his law studies in London from a wartime contract to supply yams to the army, and as soon as he qualified he was earning three times as much in a year as his training had cost him. His writings asserted the claim of the western-educated and business-oriented to take over political responsibilities from the hereditary élite, whom he somewhat unfairly caricatured as illiterate backwoodsmen; and under pressure from the 'new men', along with the conviction of the Labour Party in Britain that representative government was indispensable for econ-omic development, hereditary rulers were edged out of the political system. African governments today are no less autocratic, but their élites have come from western-style social groups – business, the professions, sometimes trade union organisations, and later from the army; an advanced level of western education has been a crucial qualification. Of course these élites become hereditary in their turn as fathers receive incomes that enable them to pay for their children's education.

It might seem absurd to generalize about an area as wide as India with all its regional differences. There would certainly be little significance in measuring the distance between the richest and the poorest inhabitants of the whole sub-continent. Such a calculation would have to be done region by region or state by state. Nevertheless, some general comments are permissible.

There were great inequalities of wealth and power in India long before the period of British rule. Invaders from the north had carved out principalities, greater or smaller, in competition with one another, and drew tribute from them which was paid in kind by villagers and converted into cash by the recipients. There were many specialist crafts, and merchants engaged in long-distance luxury trade. Under British rule, trade with Europe increased and Indians invested in industry without waiting for 'development aid'. When, in 1919, the International Labour Office was set up with a governing body to include the 'eight States of chief industrial importance', India was one of them.

Development and Indian Caste

The same kind of inequality appears in any rapidly developing country, but a type of inequality peculiar to India is that which is maintained by the caste system. Caste membership is hereditary. As it affects rural life, the essence of the system in much of India is that in any given village there is a 'dominant' caste, the members of which own most of the land, while others work it on the basis of different types of contract with the landowner, who himself works part of it with his family. In the village studied by Bailey (1957) there were a number of castes, the dominant one being the Warriors. In those studied by Epstein there were to all intents and purposes only two, Peasants and Untouchables. Each caste is associated with an occupation, though usually only a minority of the members practise it, and they are ranked in terms of the freedom of their occupation from contact with polluting substances. Lowest in the scale are the Untouchables, who have been known by other and less offensive names since Gandhi told his followers to call them 'children of God'. Since there is a list of 'untouchable' castes which are accorded certain types of legal protection, they are nowadays officially referred to as 'Scheduled Castes'; each has its own local name.

Despite the long history of economic development in India, as far as one can tell from such studies as Bailey's the ranking order of castes in any given village has remained stable until recent times (say, the last sixty or seventy years). Within that period, however, new economic opportunities have altered the distribution of wealth in India as they have in Africa. In Bailey's Bisipara (Orissa) the 'tribal' Konds, who were outside the system altogether, used to distil their own liquor until the government forbade private distilling so that it could raise excise revenue. The Hindu Distillers – a low caste because high castes do not touch spirits – grew rich selling liquor to Konds, and put their money into land. When prohibition was introduced they lost the stigma of their caste occupation, and were able to claim a status commensurate with their new wealth. The opportunity offered to Outcastes was government employment, often of a menial kind but providing them with cash incomes. They could learn to read and write, and become teachers in the schools for Kond children; or they worked as policemen, night-watchmen or office cleaners. One or two made money, but the pollution barrier was too strong for the caste as a whole to cross it. Sporadic attempts to do so led either to resistance from the 'clean' castes or to their withdrawal leaving the Outcastes alone on the field.

Nowadays, members of a single caste – high or low – form associations to pursue their collective interests, whether in economic advancement, mainly through education, or in seeking to enforce rules of conduct within the caste that will improve its status over a wider area than the village. One interpretation of the genesis of such associations is that they are organized by men with economic or political interests who obtain a following by appealing to the supposed solidarity of fellow members of a caste. It may well be that caste associations with a wide geographical spread are used as vote-getting organizations by politicians who are not greatly concerned with raising the status of their caste as such. It is true too that the symbolic behaviour by which the Outcastes were formerly required to express acceptance of their lowly status can no longer be enforced and has largely gone by the board. In the anonymous crowd of a great city people do not ask questions about caste membership.

But in smaller units it has not lost its significance. Epstein shows how, in the little manufacturing town of Mandya, members of the locally dominant caste manage to monopolise desirable employment, leaving casual labour as the only resort for the Outcastes; and how this division is not mitigated, as it used to be in the villages, by the rituals in which members of all castes, and Outcastes too, co-operated. It is no matter for surprise that the states in which Communism is strongest are those where discrimination against Outcastes has been most severe. When economists argue that 'caste' will have to be abolished before there is any hope of any successful develop-ment in India, they are presumably thinking of this kind of discrimination. As Bailey's story shows, a 'clean' caste can push its way up in the pecking order if enough of its members do well out of new opportunities. The economists' argument is rather like saying that 'race', or ethnic origin, should be abolished. Indians are born into a caste, and as long as they consider that they should marry within it, caste will continue to exist. Though governments, as in South Africa, have forbidden marriages between given categories of people, no government can *compel* people to marry against the values of their culture.

A debated question of the moment is how far inequalities of wealth and status are accepted and taken for granted, or resented and protested against, in those societies that are rapidly changing as capitalist development proceeds. Most people, no doubt, wish they were better off and envy their more prosperous fellows, but do they see the inequality as the expression of an iniquitous system, or do they find expla-nations which justify it? In other words, do the poor, or the poorer, perceive themselves as the victims of an exploitation against which they should rebel?

What has been said of India suggests that people are more interested in altering the rank order than in abolishing the ranking system. Successful competitors seek the status they think they deserve, and there is little demand that competition should be ended. What of Africa?

Attitudes towards Inequality in Africa

The Yoruba peoples of south-western Nigeria, who number ten million or more, were studied over a number of years by the anthropologist Peter Lloyd, who has devoted one of his many books (1974) to an examination of their attitude towards inequality, particularly the attitudes of the 'less equal'. His conclusions differ markedly from those of a sociologist, Gavin Williams (1974), who was associated with him in the study on which Lloyd's book is based.

The question at issue is the way in which Yoruba society is actually perceived by its 'have-not' (or 'have-less') members. Do they see it as an open one in which everyone has a change to better himself by his own efforts or as one of opposed classes in which the have-nots can hope for justice only if they combine in protest?

To begin with, although of course a census of incomes could divide the whole Yoruba population into rich and poor, the line being drawn at whatever level was chosen, the upper and lower divisions would not form *social* groups, the members of which interacted more with one another than with anyone in the other group. The most important social group is that based on descent, the lineage, and the members of any one lineage will have widely different incomes and life-styles. Within a lineage, age deserves deference independently of income. There is competition between and within lineages for the titles the holders of which traditionally were, and still largely *de facto* are, responsible for the affairs of the different towns. Popularity was an important criterion for selection; and popularity was demonstrated by the number of persons on whom the candidate had conferred favours, who would follow him about when he walked abroad and sing the praises of his generosity. Those men are generous who can afford to be; it is there that superior wealth tells. But the beneficiaries, and still more those who hope to benefit in the future, may come from all walks of life. Not all may be the great man's kin, but common kinship is regarded as a ground for solidarity and a basis for special claims. The same is true of schoolmates, who regard themselves as bound by the same solidarity as members of the traditional formally constituted age-sets. Summing up the attitudes of the Yoruba in general towards inequalities of wealth, Lloyd writes: 'Those who reach the top are deemed to have achieved their position substantially through upholding the values of Yoruba society: the successful are not seen as rising by unfair means while the honest remain poor' (1974, p. 54).

Earlier in this century the wealthy men were successful cocoa farmers, produce buyers, traders in imported goods and lorry owners. Success in these lines did not depend on formal education. Today, the highest incomes are attainable by men who have had such education and thus become qualified for appointments in a greatly expanded bureaucracy. Traditionally the ordinary Yoruba pinned his hopes on securing the patronage of a wealthy man, and many still do. Particularly in the smaller towns, an observer may see callers at such a man's house who greet him, stay a short time and depart; either they are hoping to be noticed by him and receive his patronage, or he is already their patron and they are expressing that gratitude which is a lively sense of favours to come. A Yoruba believes that his destiny, in its broad lines, is assigned him at birth; but this is not a fatalistic attitude. Up to a point one can outwit a bad destiny by one's own hard work and skill in securing a patron's favours; and a good destiny may be wasted if its possessor does not make the most of his opportunities. It is clear that there are many ambitious men in Yorubaland who make their way by means that a westerner would readily perceive as rational; it seems that destiny is apt to be seen as a matter of success of failure in finding a patron. Few of the less fortunate today have given up hope of better luck at some time in the future. People who were asked if they thought the difference in earnings between a labourer and a university graduate was unfair, replied that the latter had 'suffered' to get his education – being beaten at school and having had to put off marriage. Everyone considered self-employment – or to be an employer oneself – preferable to working for wages, but this was not because wage-earners were exploited; if people said that an employee was like a slave, all they meant was that he was under someone else's orders. In other words, they valued wealth as a source of independence and power over others rather than as an end in itself.

The patronage structure of Yoruba society as it was generally perceived linked rich and poor. Such a view is incompatible with the idea of a division between exploiting and exploited classes. As Lloyd puts it: 'We must distinguish clearly between opposition to a structure of social inequality – a belief that the basic rules governing the allocation of power and rewards should be altered – and hostility towards those in power because they are not abiding by the generally accepted rules' (1974, p. 181).

This argument repeats the long familiar distinction between revolt and revolution, perhaps made first by a courtier of Louis XVI but elevated to anthropological theory by Gluckman (1963). Williams' (1974) Marxist analysis sees the farmers' riots of 1968–70, in response to increases in taxation in a period when cocoa incomes were falling, as a 'peasant revolt', a stage in the emergence of a class consciousness that must grow until it finally leads to revolution. Peel (1980) sees this and other such movements as inherent in the relationship between any rulers and their subjects. Rulers have followers, among other reasons because they have goods to distribute, which may or may not have been extracted from their followers in the first place; in the old Yoruba kingdoms these goods came from tolls on trade, today they come from the sale of oil to foreign nations. Leaders not only have but must have followers, even in the most ruthless of dictatorships; in milder states the followers are those who consent to their authority. They make and keep followers through the distribution of the resources they control, and the followers have the sanction of protest – strikes, revolts, what you will – when they think they are not getting their fair share.

But when people resort to these sanctions it is not in pursuit of an ideal of general equality. Rather what they seek is *more* of what they are already receiving; a revolt against the level of taxation is the same demand put in negative terms. Although the farmers' riots were widespread and took the form of resort to force, it is much more often the spokesmen of territorial divisions of Nigeria, populated by representatives of many interests and income levels, who put forward demands. These divisions, once the domains of traditional political authorities, now the areas of jurisdiction of local councils, are in competition with other like divisions. *Their* demand for equality has been met by a constitution which divides Nigeria into nineteen states, all equally represented at the centre, and by the distribution of oil-earned resources in such a way that every State can have its university and its hydro-electric project. Yet within nearly every state there is a minority clamouring to be made a separate unit.

Peel argues that if 'class' action does appear, it will not be that of peasants, but of salary- and wage-earners claiming their share as individuals from their employers, the principal of whom is the Nigerian State. It would be naive to suppose that any of these are pursuing an equality that would reduce their incomes. As an economist has put it informally, 'People don't confuse a desire to be better off with a wish to be as badly off as everyone else' (Rimmer, 1981).

At present, Lloyd argues, both farmers and urban workers regard the government 'as a patron hopefully benevolent but frequently capricious' (1974, p. 214). He notes, however, that the sources of personal patronage may be drying up. Men who once valued the prestige conferred by a large following now value more the licences and contracts that are to be got from friendly relations with politicians or bureaucrats (as patrons, as clients?). Those who are making money may prefer to invest it in making more, and confine their generosity to financing the education of their close kin. The poor – or those who describe themselves as 'ordinary folk' – are indeed becoming poorer as inflation gallops, but though they have less hope of a stroke of luck, what they still value is independence and not the collective rule of the workers.

There are, then, among third world populations many different kinds of inequality and many different attitudes towards it. There may be a general deference to leaders whose legitimacy rests on tradition; if so, it may be important for development agents to get their co-operation. There may be men whose power rests on their ability to dictate the terms on which the majority of the rural population can have access to land, and who are able to thwart measures that would reduce this power. There may be people whose caste solidarity enables them to monopolise desirable employments. In these cases the problem is to find means of circumventing obstacles which would be hard to remove by direct confrontation.

Anthropologists have had less to say about the attitudes towards inequality of those who are sometimes called 'the under-privileged'. If we are interested, as I suppose most of the readers of this book will be, in development without revolution, we shall not be concerned with 'raising the consciousness' of this section of the population. Perhaps what is important for development workers of this persuasion is to avoid the assumption that people who believe in fate – or what we might prefer to call 'luck' – are neither fatalists nor Micawbers, but more like those in Britain who buy premium bonds but do not suppose that all they need do is wait for them to be drawn.

7
Enterprise and Entrepreneurs

Every improvement in technique results from the adoption by somebody, somewhere, of some new method. The individuals who make such improvements are innovators, and often loosely described as entrepreneurs. Strictly speaking the word describes a role found only in a capitalist system, which is therefore widely assumed to be more or less immoral. Yet it is not only advocates of capitalist production who discuss the presence or absence of entrepreneurship in non-industrial societies with the implication that it is a desirable quality.

The stereotype of the apathetic, fatalist peasant – or urban dweller – sunk in the inescapable 'culture of poverty' comes from Latin America. It is a description, not of all peasants or slumdwellers, but of that section of a community whose members, for whatever reason, have despaired of finding any way to improve their lot. Yet these may be the very people who have joined in peasant revolts demanding the redistribution of land when the occasion seemed to offer a chance of success. They are not, that is to say, inherently devoid of any capacity for initiative.

However, it is not so much in farming as in small-scale production and trade that entrepreneurship is sought and found. If an entrepreneur is simply an enterprising person – and this after all is what the word basically means – it is easy to find some such in a peasant community. Indeed Stavenhagen (1970) calls attention to the enterprise that can be seen among members of the Mexican *ejidos*, small-scale collective settlements most of which were created during the land reforms of 1935–40. But he adds the rider that this quality, admirable in itself, is to be deplored if it is directed to individual advancement and not to that of the collectivity as a whole.

Again, some officials of the co-operatives set up in the early days of Maoist China found that they could do better for their members by dealing with the private merchants, who at that time were still allowed to operate, than by looking to the state trading companies. This enabled them to show what, in China as anywhere else, would be called a healthy financial balance. But that was 'profit thinking' (Shue, 1980, p. 208), putting the unit towards which they had a direct obligation before the state-run economy as a whole – an abstraction that it might be hard for the most dedicated cadre to serve (except of course by abandoning the kind of initiative that is called enterprise). Evidently on some views of development the presence of initiative can be as undesirable as its absence.

Motivating Factors

Those who regard it as unequivocally to be desired, however, have advanced a number of theories, some social, some psychological, as to the circumstances in which we may expect to find it. The psychologists see the question as a matter of the upbringing of children. In some societies the adult who is most admired is set on achievement, in others the quality most highly prized is the ability to make oneself popular. Children grow up with a 'need' for achievement in the one case, for popularity in the other. An elaboration of the theory purports to predict in what sections of a society one should expect children to grow up with 'need achievement', as it is ungrammatically called. The two types have been correlated with the kind of dreams typically recorded from different ethnic groups. A contrast of this kind has been drawn between the Hausa on the one hand, and the Yoruba and Ibo on the other, in Nigeria; though it might be difficult to decide which should have the prize for entrepreneurship. The criterion chosen was the adoption of modern technical devices; but it has been cogently argued, in the case of the Hausa meat trade, that this would have no advantage over accepted methods which dispense with them.

Anthropologists, as in their wont, have found it more rewarding to look for social than psychological factors. One of these, as has been mentioned earlier, is the adoption of a new religion of a puritanical type. Norman Long (1968) studied a small population in Zambia among whom, as a matter of policy, cash-cropping had been encouraged along with plough-ing and other farming improvements. He found that by comparison with the majority, who had kept to their tradi-tional religion, an unusual number of Jehovah's Witnesses had adopted these innovations with success. In Kapepa Parish, the area studied, there were 497 adults, of whom 91 were Witnesses (47 men and 44 women). Three-quarters of these had moved away from a village where they were subject to a traditional headman, to found small independent settlements, whereas fewer than half the unconverted had done so. Twenty-four men – just half the male Witnesses – were earning cash in-comes, whereas only one-fifth of the unconverted were. Eighteen out of 49 men who had taken up tobacco were Witnesses. Over half the Witnesses had some skilled craft, only a fifth of the rest. Four-fifths of them used ploughs against a quarter of the others. Why?

The Witnesses' version of Christianity not only calls for hard work and thrift, but associates the unconverted part of mankind with the Satanic customs of a world which must be rejected *in toto*. Accordingly, most of them preferred to live away from the village where their kinsmen were clustered. The latter, if they wanted to embark on cash-crop production, could call on dependent kin, but only on them, for such additional labour as they might need, whereas the Witnesses either engaged labour on contract or made arrangements for the exchange of labour with neighbours in their small settle-ments. With them brothers really did co-operate, an ideal which is indeed universal, but is hard to attain in kin-based (or any other) societies. Whether or not the Protestant Reformation was an important factor in the rise of capitalism in Europe, it seems clear that in Africa to belong to an exclusive sect in which the members reinforce one another may be significant in encouraging entrepreneurship. An advantage, from the business point of view, of detachment from their more distant kin was that they were not asked for credit by people whom they could not refuse. They had a better reputation for reliability than non-Christians.

Clifford Geertz (1963) in his study of two Indonesian towns

defines entrepreneurship, as does B. Le Vine, in terms of the adoption of new techniques; he expressly equates 'development' with 'modernisation'. He also seeks to apply the theory that entrepreneurs will be found in sections of society which have to compensate for loss of esteem. In the Javanese town, 'Modjokuto', there had long been numbers of bazaar traders, selling goods casually acquired to casual customers and haggling over prices. They had always been despised as outsiders, as itinerant traders often are. A few of these adopted more 'western' methods of trading, setting up shops, maintaining stocks, charging fixed prices. Most of them were members of the trade reformist Masjumi movement, which, unlike orthodox Islam, makes a religious virtue of 'the systematic and untiring pursuit of worldly ends'. It does not appear to me from his account that they had recently been suffering noticeably less esteem then they always had; but they resemble Jehovah's Witnesses in their puritanical attitude to work. One of them attributed his success to work and prayer, and remarked that it took only a few minutes to pray (Geertz, 1963, p. 53).

Loss of esteem did, perhaps, play a part in 'Tabanan', the Balinese town. Here the entrepreneurs were petty princes who had lost their political power after the withdrawal of the Dutch and the revolution that followed it. Their commercial activity began in 1945, when, one might suppose, they had hardly had time to feel themselves disesteemed. Half a dozen of them combined to set up an export-import business, to which every householder under their authority (so they did still have authority) contributed capital, seemingly without compulsion. The business was organised by utilising a traditional group, the *seka*, which might be based on any common interest – common membership of a village, perhaps, or common use of single irrigation source. The *seka*, says Geertz, had been capable of innovation. One, for example, sold some rice-land to buy a school bus, calculating that there was more future in education than in rice farming; this calculation has been made in most LDCs, even if it has not led to much purchase of buses. The shareholders of the new business were organised in *seka* of twenty members each, and the business, taking the name People's Trade Association, got from the military government a monopoly of coffee buying in Bali and a contract to supply rice to all the prisons in the island. Can some other factor besides business acumen as normally understood have been operative here?

Abner Cohen's study (1969) of the Hausa businessmen who control the north-south trade both in meat and in kola nuts in Nigeria does not ask what social circumstances prompted them to embark on their activity. Perhaps their forebears started, eighty years or so ago, as peddlers like those of Modjokuto; does it matter? Needing a base in Ibadan, they were astute enough to capitalise on the Yoruba idea that foreigners, assumed to be thieves and vagabonds, ought to be confined to a kind of ghetto, and on the British idea that different ethnic groups should be allowed to follow 'their own customs' under local authorities legitimised by their own tradition. Within the Sabon Gari (stranger city) they built up an entirely non-traditional political system, which rested on the control of accommodation for travellers by a few large landlords and the prohibition for members of Sabo of any co-operation with the Yoruba. In itself this showed some genius for organisation as well as innovation.

Cohen does not find the origin of their interest in large-scale trade in any form of religion, but he does show how affiliation to a minority Islamic community became an instrument for the maintenance of a political authority which lost the support that the British had given it when Nigeria became independent. But the importance of the Tijaniyya was that it emphasised the strict observance of ritual as a ground for superiority, not that it called for devotion to hard work.

Cohen also examines the assertion that the Hausa leaders lack the innovative qualities of their Yoruba neighbours. Certainly they have not taken to transporting their cattle by train, nor do they lodge their takings in the bank, but is this because they do not see the advantages of these modern devices? Least of all can it be a reflection of 'Islamic obedience versus Christian individualism' (Le Vine, 1966, p. 84). For a number of reasons, at the time of Cohen's study, it could often be more efficient to have cattle driven south on the hoof than transported by rail. Only a limited number of wagons were available, and there was often a wait of several days for them. Sometimes the whole rail system was disrupted by floods.

Money in a bank can only be drawn out at stated times, and dealers from the north may want to leave at some other time, perhaps in the middle of the night, so they must entrust their money to the landlord for safe keeping, and the landlord must have it on hand. They do not use cheques because they frequently have to make payments to semi-literate people. Indeed this story is a convincing argument for 'appropriate technology'.

No one denies that enterprise is a scarce social resource. But it does not seem very profitable to assume that it is a characteristic of groups rather than of individuals. Like other rare qualities, it may appear anywhere, though some social circumstances may be more propitious than others for its development.

The Small Entrepreneur

Moreover, as Marris and Somerset (1971) point out in the context of Nairobi, what a superficial observer takes for lack of initiative may in fact be insufficient familiarity with the techniques of modern business (in circumstances where these are necessary for success, as they are not in the Nigerian meat trade). There is, for most small businessmen, a point beyond which they cannot expand if one man has to supervise the whole organisation. Yet unless they expand they cannot compete with the larger enterprises that have been before them in the field. Indeed, at this stage one might well say that it is not so much invention as imitation that is needed – imitation of the kind of organisation in which supervisory functions are delegated, so that the manager need not try to be 'everywhere at once'. It may well be that the same dislike of being ordered about that prompts the Kenya businessman to strike out on his own may deter others from becoming his subordinates. The members of an African religious sect in Zimbabwe, the Makowe Vapostori (Apostles), are independent craftsmen relying entirely on their income from selling their own products, because, as they believe along with the People's Democracies, it is wrong to employ labour. So the spirit of entrepreneurship is not enough by itself to guarantee the appearance of a locally-based big business.

It seems that there is a cut-off point at which there is nothing in his experience for the African businessman to build on if he wants to compete with rivals from other continents. More than one African government has thought that all that need be done was to expel the competitors, and then has found that to take over a business and to manage it are very different things. One difficulty is that the small businessman depends for supplies on the big businessman with his foreign contacts and his established goodwill. The contacts are broken by the expulsion of the expatriates, and again the African business-man comes to a cut-off point.

Yet the small entrepreneur is not to be sneezed at. His innovations have often increased the amenities of village life. In an Indian sugar-growing area there are cane-crushers driven by bullocks in many villages (and they must have been innov-ations at some time). Then someone with a small surplus installs a mechanical one, at the same time agitating (and partly paying) for the extension of electric power to the village. Not all the villagers can afford to have it in their houses, but they are all glad of street lighting at night; and in homes that can afford it, children can do their homework after dark. A grain mill can do in a few minutes what used to take a woman three or four hours of arduous work. A recent example of actual invention is on record from Bihar, where a farmer devised a means of constructing a tube-well for irrigation out of bamboo and coir, at much lower cost than that of the materials supplied by the government, and he or another had the entrepreneurship to bolt a diesel pump to an ox-cart so that it could be moved from one well to another and the owner could hire it out.

The study *African Businessmen*, made by Marris and Somerset (1971), of businessmen in Nairobi collected individual histories and found that they ran a typical course, but, except in so far as they were predominantly Kikuyu, they could not be described as coming from a particular dis-esteemed group. A youth would begin as an employee, probably of an Asian, in, say, a car-repairing business. There he would pick up the requisite skills, and when he had saved a little money he would set up on his own, hiring a piece of pavement to sit on and mend bicycles. If this succeeded he would rent a shop, and in time he might have a dozen or more men working for him. He would try to impose strict discipline on them, and sometimes succeed, fining any who came late to work and insisting on the repayment of all sums unaccounted for. Very seldom was such a man willing to employ a subordinate to whom he could delegate responsibility. 'If he is as clever as you are he will cheat you', said one. But unless the entrepreneur will delegate, he cannot expand his business to a size sufficient to compete with the larger firms already in the field. Instead, those who make a profit commonly start another business small enough for one-man control – and then they must try to be in two places at once, and both enterprises are liable to suffer.

The Nairobi businessmen do not seem to have been inspired by any particular religious movement; if they had been they might have found themselves in a community among whom there was mutual confidence. They are not subject to any rule such as that which requires the Jehovah's Witnesses to repudiate their unconverted kin. Instead they have had, each for himself, to teach the latter that 'kinsmen are not in business to support their relatives'. The obligations of kinship that can be met by sharing the grain in the store cannot be translated into a wife's right to take goods from stock or a brother's to treat a loan as a gift. Many of the men interviewed had sad stories of their attempts to employ brothers who considered themselves exempt from the rules of business dealing; sometimes a refusal to give a kinsman special terms was ascribed to resentment over an old family quarrel, which would then flare up again.

So Nairobi's small businessmen tend to become estranged from their kin. But they cannot aspire to membership of the new élite, whose status rests on their western-style education. Indeed it is in relation to them that the entrepreneurs are dis-esteemed, and if they are consequently activated by 'need achievement', the need is to demonstrate that they too can make a contribution to the advancement of their country. To be rich is not by itself enough for the status they are seeking. So, although they are not – and hardly can be – very generous employers, they do identify their activities with the welfare of their workers and of the community, as others have before them. 'Entrepreneurship', said one of them, 'expresses the spirit of African socialism' (Marris and Somerset, 1971, p. 226).

Marris and Somerset suggest various ways in which the government agency intended to help small businessmen could be more effective. Instead of offering text-book courses on book-keeping, an art they have usually learned by doing, or on management based on American experience, it could give technical training directly related to market opportunities, and it could provide a market advisory service. It could organize discussions between businessmen and representatives of the institutions with which they have to deal – banks, overseas companies, commercial attachés. These could lead to the recognition of a commercial ethic that would be widely enough accepted for trust to replace the present general suspicion. It would also be helpful to give businessmen a clearer understanding of their legal responsibilities. Again, the government might invest in promising enterprises instead of offering credit.

Finally, the two writers comment on the kind of contradictory actions of those in authority that spring from inadequate co-ordination. A businessman is given a loan, but cannot get from the appropriate agency the supplies for which he has the credit. An industrial estate is built for new enterprises which cannot develop without protection, but government policy is opposed to protection. Public agencies, of which there are many, do not buy from Africans when they might.

African Businessmen is the work of a sociologist and an economist in collaboration. It shows how much practical advice can come from close study at 'platoon level'. We do not know how much of it has been taken.

The Informal Sector

The framers of urban development schemes have tended to be hostile to the small entrepreneur. To the compilers of statistics such men (or women) are unpersons or at best nonpersons; that is to say, there is no place for them in records which define employment as wage labour and a business as one employing a sufficient number of people for labour legislation to apply to it. Their activities do, however, fall into a recognized category, the 'informal sector', a term introduced in

1972 in an ILO report on employment in Kenya, and this is the sector which is expanding most rapidly in the expanding cities. To those who equate 'development' with 'modernization' and 'modernization' with large-scale production, their existence is deplorable. An adviser on urban development in Delhi wrote:

> A great proportion of the activities undertaken in cities are parasitic and these parasitic activities should be dispensed with. . . In so far as this activity is wasteful, competitive and unhealthy, it may be controlled by other measures, and the productive resources thus released might be devoted to other purposes more in accord with Indian desires. [What Indians, what desires? The productive resource most significant here is initiative.] And later the main source of parasitism is the overwhelming inefficiency of petty trade, petty services and petty manufacturing, and the tremendous following population which this inefficiency implies for any vital and central activity in the urban scene. (Harris 1961)

In other words, only those who work in large factories contribute to production. More recently some economists have come to welcome the 'informal sector' precisely because it is labour intensive, and would invest resources in encouraging it. At the same time they remark that labour power is wasted when such enterprises do not do enough business for those engaged in them to work full-time. As in so many instances discussed in this book, the question is to find out where this is, or is not, the case. Lloyd (1979, p. 46) pointedly observes: 'Officially fully employed is the messenger who sits idly in the office corridor for most of the day save when told to fetch a file or a cup of tea . . . In every society 'people are under-employed in the sense that with improved tools their output would be higher.'

It is largely anthropologists who, through their intensive study of small communities, have recognized the wide diversity of 'informal' activities as well as the differences in the size of enterprises falling under this head. They have looked at the picture from the actor's point of view (Lloyd, 1979, ch. 3) rather than the onlooker's, and have asked whether individuals make their living in the informal sector merely because they have failed to get wage employment or to rise in such employment, or because they prefer it.

An economist would draw a distinction between the small-scale producers of goods for sale to larger manufacturers or retailers and those who provide goods and services for their immediate neighbours. In Singapore, the former include makers of nuts and bolts, concrete bars and furniture. In Nairobi (Lloyd, 1979) they make front guards and carriers for bicycles, and fashionable dress-shops put out work to individual tailors and seamstresses. It is these small-scale entrepreneurs too who are called in as 'handymen' for all kinds of repairs in the houses of the well-to-do. In this sense the informal sector depends on the development of the formal.

But by far the greater number of 'informal' entrepreneurs are those who produce for a local clientele, and if their work is 'petty' it is commensurate with the incomes of the customers. Nevertheless, Lloyd observes that a self-employed man may well earn more than the legal minimum wage, which in many countries is not enough to cover the cost of living, and that some of them in the Yoruba towns have incomes equal to all but the most successful cocoa growers (this was written at a time when cocoa was flourishing). They include petty traders, who may display their goods on stalls in front of their houses or by the side of roads. Attempts are made to limit their numbers by requiring them to be licensed, since trade, not being directly productive, is held to be parasitic (only small-scale trade, it appears). The 'petty services' offered include bicycle hire, taxis, barbering, shoe-shine, prostitution. But the small-scale producers include some, the goldsmiths for example, who in other contexts would be called craftsmen, a term of approval. Tailors make up lengths of cloth brought by their customers into shirts and trousers, or make the elaborately embroidered gowns of Yoruba and Hausa. Nowadays carpenters and shoemakers use modern tools. Machines can do the embroidery, and silk and cotton thread is bought in the big stores by middlemen who first supply it to weavers, and then buy their output and sell it to these same stores (the middlemen themselves members of the informal sector). Most of these people 'serve the poor' not only in the sense that they provide services, but that they produce goods at lower cost than the larger businesses.

They do so by evading the constraints imposed in the formal sector, on living conditions, on wórking hours, on rates of pay, on liability to tax. Working conditions have been imposed in the rich countries to protect employees from exploitation, and governments in the LDCs naturally aim to impose the same standards. But a great many of those countries' less educated young men look forward to practising a trade that they have learnt, independently or as small employers, and do not regard the protection offered to wage earners as compensation for what they see as a loss of independence. While radical writers see the informal sector as a sort of dustbin for the unemployed, those who do not succeed in it are apt to see *themselves* as 'forced into wage labour' (Lloyd, 1974, p. 111), and will stay in employment only until they have saved enough to try again. One reason, no doubt, is that the wage earners, however often they have been called an 'aristocracy', have not in fact been able to demand a level of wages higher than the income of a successful independent entrepreneur. It is among the latter, indeed, that is found the initiative so often mentioned as a prerequisite for development.

An economist who has looked more closely at this aspect of the LDCs (Elkan, 1978) than many in his profession sums up the situation in these words:

> Governments are inclined to believe that things produced in 'modern' hygienic factories must do more to promote development. This is mistaken economic analysis. Things produced with simple implements and in premises that may consist of no more than a tin roof on wooden poles economize on fixed capital, if nothing else. Arguably they may absorb more units per unit of output, but some of these units, like discarded tins or tyres, would have no alternative uses whilst the people working in the concerns manifestly lack alternative employment opportunities yielding higher incomes. There is also a clear market for the things produced or these activities would not take place. To discriminate against such activities is to mistake the symptoms of poverty for their cause. The informal sector exists because countries are poor; it helps to reduce their poverty, by providing employment and a source of income to those who have no

better alternative. It is not easy to see what governments could do actively to promote this form of economic activity, but they could at least refrain from harrassing those whose livelihoods depend upon it. (Elkan, 1978, p. 141)

8

Man-made Lakes and Resettlement

The processes commonly described as settlement and resettlement (relocation, translocation) are both movements of population. Settlement is also sometimes called colonization, a word
which implies movement into areas which have not previously
been inhabited or cultivated. All resettlement, however, is not
movement into uninhabited areas, and one of its problems is
the relations between newcomers and existing inhabitants.
Movement may be spontaneous, when, for example, an
extension of communications brings some region within reach
of markets, or irrigation comes to areas that previously
depended on an uncertain rainfall. People who have not lost
their homes can hardly be directed to settle elsewhere, but they
may be encouraged to do so, and the conditions under which
they settle in specified places may be laid down in greater or less
detail. Settlement in areas expected to be more attractive than
the settlers' original homes has been promoted on a small scale
in Africa, and on a much larger scale in Latin America, where
one motive for the authorities has sometimes been the establishment of a population in frontier areas (Nelson, 1973).

Displaced Populations

Re-settlement is a matter of providing for people who have
been made homeless, and in these days there are two major
reasons for them to be so. One is the construction of dams,
creating lakes which always submerge the homes of thousands
of people; the aim is always to provide electricity for industrial
development, but this may be combined with irrigation
schemes. The other is war or political upheaval, in which
people are either driven from their homes or run away without

waiting to be driven. A crucial difference between the two categories of homeless is that the first *cannot* return, whereas the second may go on for many years hoping that eventually they may be able to go home, and the governments that have taken them in may entertain the same hopes. Only the second, curiously enough, are formally described as 'displaced persons'.

A recent calculation (Scudder, 1975) has given the following figures for populations displaced by the creation of man-made lakes: Zambia and Zimbabwe (the Kariba Dam) 56,000; Ghana (the Volta Dam) 70,000; Nigeria (the Kainji Dam) 42,000; Ivory Coast (the Kossou Dam) possibly over 80,000; Egypt and Sudan (the Aswan Dam) 100,000, some of whom have had to move several times as more and more water was impounded; Turkey (the Keban Dam) up to 30,000; in Thailand about 30,000 peasants were 'relocated' when a dam was built on a tributary of the Mekong River, and ten times as many will lose their homes if the main river is dammed. 'Looking to the future', says Scudder, 'we can expect the construction of large-scale dams to continue, along with the relocation of hundreds of thousands of people' (1975, p. 454). The latest (1980) candidate for the largest power scheme in the world is the Itaipu Dam on the Brazil-Paraguay frontier. *The Times* (23 July 1980) assures us that this is being built 'tightly to schedule', but does not mention any human beings on the site.

It is well recognized by now that to lose one's home is a deeply disturbing experience, almost equivalent to the loss of a loved person. It is also recognized that most people 'get over' such losses in time. Impatient dambuilders are only too likely to take for granted that, whatever the original upheaval, 'they'll shake down in the long run'. The Gwembe Tonga, from whom Scudder got his first acquaintance with resettlement, have indeed shaken down, and in a shorter run than that in which, as Keynes so wisely reminded us, 'we are all dead'. Perhaps the Vietnamese, and now the Cuban, boat people, those who survive, will shake down into some kind of tolerable life. But anyone who still believes in avoiding the infliction of unnecessary suffering should want to know how this could have been avoided in earlier 'relocation' exercises, or could be in future ones.

The Kariba Dam

As was indicated in Chapter 1, the paradigm for the anthropological study of this problem is the exhaustive investigation of a sample of Gwembe villages made by Colson and Scudder (Colson, 1971). In this instance three kinds of errors were made. One was the decision taken, *after* the preparations for the move had begun, first to raise the level of the water and then to advance the date when the dam would close. Another was a matter of organization in which ignorance of what would be needed was compounded by too high an estimate of the resources of the technical departments of government. The third was the direct result of failure to understand the circumstances of Gwembe life, their seasonal programme of activities, the division of labour between men, young and old, and women, and their rules regarding the transmission of property.

When the purpose of dam building is the generation of electricity rather than the control of water for the improvement of agriculture (as it is with all large dams), the direct benefits from it go to others than the population which it displaces. It may be argued that they will gain from the general increase in productivity, and indeed some do gain from new opportunities of urban employment. The Kariba Dam was to have been the economic foundation of a European-governed Central African Federation, of which the political basis was the federation of the (then) two Rhodesias and Nyasaland. The federation was dissolved less than five years after the new Kariba Lake was filled. The political climate of its inception was not favourable to serious concern for African interests. But it is worth asking how much, and what kind of, thought is given, in the newly independent countries, to the peasants who have to leave their homes. In an example to be discussed later, there was a good deal, and yet the benefits of resettlement fell far short of what had been intended.

In the Gwembe country that Colson and Scudder studied, the District Officers – the Administrative officials in direct contact with the Africans – were deeply concerned for the people's welfare. They could not allow them to choose whether they would stay or move, but they did everything possible to let them choose where they would go. Then came the technical decision to raise the level of the lake so that the new homes they had chosen would be flooded. The Africans could understand only that they had been deceived; they did not know who it was that had betrayed them. From that moment all confidence in the goodwill or good faith of the administration was lost. One must hope that this was a unique event. But when one reads that in Brazil the construction of the dam for a major hydro-electric project was approved by the World Bank and actually begun before any thought had been given to plans for re-settlement (Scudder, 1980), one must feel that it is risky to hope too much.

Colson and Scudder followed the experiences of their sample villagers in detail. The stories of different villages were by no means identical; some were much happier than others. If I concentrate on the disasters, it is because they are what anthropological knowledge might help to prevent on later occasions.

The worst hardships were suffered by 6,000 people who could not go to the sites they had chosen because under the new plan they would be flooded. These people were sent instead to the Lusitu plateau, a sparsely inhabited area a hundred miles from their homes. Among the promises made them was an assurance that water supplies would be provided in advance and maintained by the government. The Water Department, which was responsible, proposed to do this by digging wells and boreholes. They could not, or did not, make enough manpower and machinery available, and, in addition, they did not know that the underground water in that region would prove to be undrinkable. Eventually the government made arrangements to bring water by pipe from the Zambezi; and these proved so satisfactory that they have been gradually extended over the Lusitu area. If this had been done in the first place money would not have been wasted on useless boreholes, thousands of people would not have had to live for several years with inadequate water, and possibly the lives lost in an epidemic of dysentery would have been saved (Scudder, 1975). Here the technical knowledge that was lacking was not that of anthropologists. But anthropologists would have had some-thing to say about the arrangements for the actual move. For those who had to move a long distance (a hundred miles) lorry transport was provided for a single journey, to be made on one day. Of course the Public Works Department could hardly have been expected to run a taxi service. But they assumed that the 'bush' Gwembe had no property apart from their livestock, and the stores of grain, tobacco bundled for sale, pots and pans, mats and stools, ploughs, and so on, had to be left behind and collected later (not by the owners, who were not allowed to go home lest they should refuse to move again). Many breakables were broken, and valued property saved for the start of the new life was lost.

The anthropologist has most to say, however, about misconceptions as to people's organization of their time and their division of labour. The men, as was mentioned, were sent ahead to prepare the new homesteads during the dry season, when, it was supposed, they had nothing to do at home. This was a government order, which most of them obeyed. But at home too this was the season for clearing the fields and building or repairing houses. For the younger men it was also the season when they sought employment to earn cash for, among other things, paying taxes. The 'opportunity cost', as economists call it, of unpaid building work was unusally high, since paid labour, actually in connection with preparations for the move, was offered nearer home.

Moreover, it was assumed that housebuilding was entirely men's work, whereas there was a clear division of labour: men cut the poles for walls, put them in place and thatched the roofs, women cut the thatching grass and slapped the mud on the framework. But women had never been called up as men were, and they had work at home. They had to prepare fields there for the final planting before the move; they had to see that sheep and goats were secured at night from the raids of hyenas. So such building as was done in advance was done reluctantly, by men only, and often abandoned before it was finished.

The promise of compensation to individuals for losses caused by the move was kept, but the payments did not go to those who should have received them in terms of Gwembe conceptions of property. The Gwembe belong to that minority of the world's population who inherit property in the female line – from the mother's descent group and not the father's.

But with the vast majority of the world's population they believe that a man is the head of his household and has authority over everyone living in it. It is a rule among the Gwembe that when a young man first marries he must build his hut in the homestead of an older relative, any such relative, therefore not one with whom he shares common claims on property. One element in the compensation payment was for the loss of housing in the home villages. For this purpose the number of huts in a homestead was counted, and a lump sum paid to the head. Although his younger dependants were regarded as the owners of the huts they had built, they received nothing. In addition, a fixed sum was awarded to each individual, even small children, and this again was paid as a lump sum to the head of a family group, often including his extra-familial dependents. (Admittedly, it would have been impossible without some form of trust to allot individual sums to minors.) Most of the recipients shared out a part of the money paid them, but none shared equally with the other family members. This was a source of much resentment on the part of younger men, even including some who in later years claimed to have 'worked for' their fathers simply by being assessed for compensation as infants.

Paradoxically, these windfalls for a minority led to an increase in the number of Gwembe entrepreneurs. Some of the older men who acquired substantial sums invested in ploughs, trained oxen and ox-carts, and maize grinders, which they used themselves, and fishing boats and nets which their sons used; or they set up stores. The grievance of young men in a system where they are expected to work at increasing property that they will not inherit is permanent, and this expression of it was only temporary. So one might say that it all worked out for the best. But is that a reason not to care about getting the facts right?

The Volta Move

The resettlement plans for the Volta Dam in Ghana (Chambers, 1970) did not disregard the interests of the population to be displaced. On the contrary, the Prime

Minister, Kwame Nkrumah, publicly stated that no one should be worse off as a result of the move, and all the government departments in turn sought to improve the standard of living of the transplanted persons, each on the lines of its own speciality. Whereas the Kariba move had offered nothing beyond a minimal infrastructure – roads which were in fact built and wells which were not – the Volta move provided for government assistance on a large scale. In the eyes of those who believe that self-help leads to the most satisfactory accommodation to new surroundings, this was a mistake of principle. In practice it had the disadvantage that more was promised than resources and organization could produce.

The move was to be preceded by a detailed social survey which, it was calculated, would need four years. But after this had been decided upon, difficulties arose about the financing of the project, and when agreement was reached, after four years of uncertainty, the survey had to be a crash exercise; in spite of this it was by no means useless.

Unlike the Gwembe, the people involved here would be moving into an area already fairly densely populated. Unlike the Gwembe too, they differed in language and culture both among themselves and, in many cases, from those who were to be their 'hosts'. They were not to find their own homesteads and fields in unoccupied areas, but, so as to enjoy the modern style amenities that were planned for them, to be grouped in townships where the government would provide houses of approved type. The inhabitants of 700 small villages were concentrated in 52 of these townships. They were not very large; the largest was designed for an initial population of 5,500, and the smallest had only 14 houses. The average population was to be 1,320. These differences reflect a policy which allowed people within broad limits to choose both their home and their new neighbours, and there is no record of refusal to move; nor were there any last minute changes of plan which could lead to imputations of bad faith. The move took place in 1964.

Housing itself, however, produced the worst difficulties. At an early stage it had been proposed that people should build their own houses, as they did at Kariba, but that they should be required to meet a minimum standard. Later it was realized that there would be no time for this. As a compromise with the principle of self-help, and in recognition of the fact that a Ghanaian family expands not by building additional dwellings as in Kariba, but by adding new rooms to a basic construction, each family was given a 'core' house with concrete floors and aluminium roof, but walls for only one room. They were to build the other walls themselves, and the plots would be large enough to make further additions later. But in the meantime the whole family, whatever its members and whatever the relationship between the members, had to sleep in one room; they might be fifteen or more. And the minimum standard of new construction was still the rule, while most people could not afford cement blocks even when they could get the cement. Inevitably they set up 'unauthorised structures', sometimes using materials from their old homes. The 'beautifully designed new townships' were turning into slums. Sometimes people were made to demolish these genuinely self-help additions. Eventually the rules were relaxed.

Although villages were being concentrated in townships, their inhabitants were still farmers. The Ghanaian government had embarked on a national plan for the improvement of productivity in agriculture, based on co-operative farming with mechanized clearing of land and a fixed rotation of crops This was applied to the new settlements, and farmers could be evicted from their holdings if they did not follow it. Much of this book has been concerned with the difficulties of imposing technical solutions to farming problems in ignorance of the social organization of the farmers. Here they were compounded by the failure of those responsible to produce the necessary equipment, particularly tractors, in time, or at all; and this was itself not simply a technical matter, but the result of giving responsibility for the supply to a political body, the United Ghana Farmers' Co-operative Council, who were to all intents and purposes amateurs. As the Gwembe had arrived to find their new homes waterless, many of the Volta settlers found that the cleared farm plots they had been promised were still under forest and bush much denser than any in Zambia. Many of them left the settlements for more profitable activities elsewhere – fishing in the new lake, market gardening on its shores, traditional farming on vacant land bought from the chiefs in whose area it lay. As late as 1972 hardly any of the settlements were fully occupied.

The Volta planners had foreseen another problem which those of Zambia had not; that the newcomers would not be welcomed by those already living in the neighbourhoods to which they were sent. As seems to be a common reaction to the stresses set up by a wholesale move, there was an unusual number of deaths in the first months of the arrival of the Gwembe in Lusitu. There was a special cause for this, moreover; numbers of women and children were seized with a sickness that seems to have been caused by eating some wild vegetable that they did not know was poisonous; men, who do not forage for food, did not suffer. So there were many occasions for those death rituals which give the survivors confidence in the continuity of life. But the Gwembe rituals involve drumming, and the 'host population' would not allow this. And other rituals could not be performed because the local ritual specialists claimed a monopoly. The Volta settlers were allowed to choose their new homes near ethnically similar populations, but with small minority groups this was not always possible. It was assumed, or at least hoped, that the newcomers would be 'absorbed', and that the new amenities which were planned – but alas, not always provided – would benefit all alike, and reconcile the 'host communities' to the influx. In fact, as has happened in many another scheme, the 'hosts' resented what they perceived as unfair privileges granted to the immigrants. In some places new settlers were actually chased off land their right to which was not recognized. This last difficulty had again been foreseen, but there had been no time to deal with the legal aspects of land rights before the move had to be made.

Needs to be Met

On the basis of his work in Zambia and of a number of later studies by himself and others, Scudder (1975, 1980) has set out a number of considerations that anyone planning a relocation exercise should bear in mind, and has recommended them to the World Bank, after being invited to consider settlement projects for which its aid was sought. Whereas another writer (Nelson, 1973) has urged that the delay needed for a preliminary investigation must be included in the cost of a project and so cannot be allowed to go on too long, Scudder argues that there is no substitute for a thorough initial study. This of course involves data that must be supplied by specialists in other fields than anthropology. Scudder offers an illuminating model of the kind of collaboration between specialisms that would be fruitful. In addition to agronomic and hydrological surveys, there should be a study by 'two experts in the behavioral and social sciences – one with local expertise and the other with topical expertise dealing with resettlement'. He gives high priority to water supplies, observing, first that they are very often poor at a short distance from the rivers being dammed, second, that if an area is sparsely populated and so available for new settlement, this is probably because its water supply is poor, and, third, that not only initial installation but permanent maintenance must be provided for. In one of the Volta settlement areas, ten years after the move people in one of the villages were getting their water from scooped-out holes in a streambed because a pump had first broken down and then been taken away.

Scudder's thesis is that settlement authorities must recognize a transition period between what might be called uprooting – and is always resisted as long as resistance is possible – and re-rooting. During this period the people being moved are under stress for many different reasons. He calls them 'relocatees', a word which pungently reminds a reader that they do not move of their own volition. Because they are sentient beings and not plants, the uprooting period begins in practice with he first knowledge, even rumour, that a move is threatened, and it lasts until they 'regain economic self-sufficiency in their new habitat' and 'begin to feel at home with both the natural environment and the hosts' (1975, p. 456). This period will last at least as much as two years and may be ten or more. People are not only baffled by their new surroundings but they grieve for their old ones. The women in Lusitu longed for the little alluvial gardens that had come down to them from their kin over the generations. Both men and women regretted being separated from the graves of their forefathers, and this for more than sentimental reasons. Burial places are symbols of the unity of the kin group, and of its continuity, places of the dead though they be. Then there are rituals to guarantee the success of planting. The Gwembe performed these at the neighbourhood shrines that they had left behind, and at first they could find no substitute for them. To re-establish such rites, as the Gwembe did in the end, is as much a part of coming to terms with the new environment as are more material matters such as finding which wild plants are edible. These aspects of resettlement can hardly be dealt with by political action; they must simply be recognized as adding to those stresses which *can* be relieved by suitable organization of the move.

In Scudder's view there must inevitably be a period during which the 'relocatees' will depend on outside sources of food – today usually the World Food Program. Effective planning would make this as short as could be, and would, if possible, arrange that the basic food supplied be familiar to the recipients, or at least something that they can cook by their accustomed methods. People may have stores of grain to bring with them; though during the Lusitu move many of these were lost in the clumsy loading of the trucks. Sometimes they are warned not to plant the fields that they are leaving (either because they are actually about to be flooded or so that nobody will be tempted to come back from the new home), and sometimes, as in the Volta case, they are told to get rid of their livestock. Thus they may begin their new life with seriously depleted resources. Scudder recommends that agricultural production should be kept up until the last moment, and restarted in the new settlement as soon as possible; this implies that the movement be made between the harvest in the old home and the time for planting in the new, and that some land must be cleared in advance. In Lusitu, provision was indeed made for the latter, but it was inadequate for the contingent reasons that have been mentioned.

But to plan the optimum conditions for a short transition period is not the same as assuming that what Scudder calls the period of potential growth should begin at the moment when the settlers arrive on the new site. It was this haste, this laudable desire to introduce them immediately to a new and better world, that was the bane of the Volta scheme. Instead of concentrating on the number and quality of houses to be built, governments should give first priority to the 'economic and socio-cultural viability' of the new communities they are seeking to create. They should begin with infrastructure – water supplies 'at the right time in the right amounts in properly designed, constructed and maintained canals', roads to transplant produce and centres to market it. Sometimes, he remarks, there is already a market within reach of the new settlement, yet the latter is treated as though it existed in isolation. (One recalls, Chapter 5, the new market outside Katsina described by Polly Hill, which completely failed to replace the local women's 'house trade'.) And what is *most important* for the success of a settlement is that the newcomers *should want to go on living there.*

A viable community must be one in which the members have permanent and satisfactory contacts – a metaphorical 'anchor'. 'Relocatees' are moved from such communities; hence their resistance. At the very least, efforts can be made to resettle them as communities. Then arises their relationship with the 'hosts', who, as has been mentioned, see them as unfairly privileged intruders, not as sufferers in need of relief. It is now the World Bank's policy to urge 'equitable treatment' for both sections of the newly created community.

Governments committed to land reform often disapprove of spontaneous settlement, which, as Scudder points out, has been the main response to population expansion all over the world, and is by definition undertaken by people interested in new opportunities. Thier action is called by pejorative terms such as 'squatting' (not pejorative in Australia, however; it all depends who does it). Botswana uses the original word 'self-allocation'.

But spontaneous settlement can be kept under a measure of government control, if holdings are offered to individuals selected by the authorities on the grounds of their farming efficiency or other criteria.

In settlements of this kind there is often a high turnover of plotholders, and where land has been redistributed in reform schemes (see Chapter 4), the new holders are often found to take little interest in working their land under the organization imposed on them. Scudder makes two comments here. The first is that, if settlers spend their time in activities other than farming – cattleraising, for example, or even off-farm activities – this is a sign of that entrepreneurship which, though it is condemned in some countries, is not seen askance by the World Bank. These activities can be a source of accumulation that will lead to investment in farming later on. Second, he says that any viable community should have a reasonable number of members who are not farmers. Some schemes, for example in the Jordan Valley, allow for fewer than one non-farming to every farming family; Scudder calculates that a successful scheme can support more non-farmers than farmers.

Finally, a question too little considered is the effect of river projects on the populations who are *not* re-settled. When a river is dammed, its level is controlled by the use of sluices. It no longer floods in the rainy season. Farmers on the banks should be, and sometimes are, compensated by irrigation works. But others besides them may have depended on the annual flood. Below the Kainji Dam on the Niger hundreds of thousands of people have lost the livelihood they gained from fishing in the flood waters, and fishing production has been halved. Yam and rice production have fallen too, and there is no dry season grazing for livestock. And this is the outcome of a scheme to alleviate poverty.

9

Cities and Slums

The enormous recent increase in the population of cities all over the LDCs is a commonplace. It is not an aim of development policies, far from it; it is an unintended consequence. It presents governments with problems of various kinds, notably that of providing adequate housing. Some of them also think these problems cannot be solved unless the flow of migration is controlled. This was one reason, though only a minor one, why Chairman Mao banished thousands of city dwellers to the country to 'learn from the peasants' in the Great Proletarian Cultural Revolution; it is one reason, though perhaps a minor one, for the South African policy of 'influx control' aimed at limiting the African population of cities strictly to the numbers for which there is employment. In that country, when it was first introduced by a relatively liberal government, it was a reaction to the devastation of the 1918 influenza epidemic; it was recognized that reasonably sanitary housing conditions must be provided for urban labourers, and at the same time that the resources available for this would be limited. Of course the fear that epidemics starting in slums will spread to high-income areas reinforces or may even take precedence over humanitarian considerations.

Many studies of urbanization have been made by demographers. They are interested in people not as individuals attached to social and cultural values, but as units to be grouped in categories by such criteria as age, sex, marital status, region of origin, length of residence in the city. Perhaps their main practical significance is in forecasting rates of increase and so indicating the likely future demands on resources. Valuable as is their information, it tells us little of the reactions of newcomers to a city to policies designed on the one hand to do them good, and on the other to keep them in order. It is well recognized that many city dwellers live in conditions

121

even less sanitary than those they have left behind, notably in their exposure to epidemics; and that there is more theft and violence in urban areas, simply because it is easier for crime to go undetected. Indeed the stereotype of the wicked city may well be current in the villages from which the migrants come. It is also widely believed today that the frustrations of slum dwellers may express themselves in revolution, and this is another reason for trying either to improve their lot or to control them, perhaps both at once. Certainly some kinds of frustration express themselves in rioting, as people in British cities have reason to know; though there may also be rioting which does not orginate in any obvious frustration.

Migrants to Cities

Urban renewal projects are among those sponsored by international aid agencies, and an anthropologist would ask here what exactly has been planned, or has been done; how that has affected the people involved, and what has been their reaction. An essential point to begin with is that the recent migrants to cities are not rootless individuals to be manipulated at will, whether by 'rabble-rousers' or by authorities 'relocating' them in slum clearance schemes. Nor can they be 'integrated' by allotting houses in strict order or application, as I once saw someone planning to do in Nigeria, and as is apparently the policy of Singapore, with its far deeper splits between Chinese and Malays and its municipal accommodation 'filled up on a multi-racial basis' (Gamer, 1972). Communities grow out of the interaction of individuals, but they cannot be compelled to interact by knocking their heads together.

A number of anthropologists have put on record what, indeed, could have been predicted by the exercise of a little imaginative commonsense. Newcomers to a city do not hurl themselves into a void; each one seeks out, or even travels with, a neighbour or kinsman who looks after him until he has found his feet. Where a city draws migrants from different directions, as did Stanleyville (now Lubumbashi) in Belgian days, there will be a concentration in any given quarter of people who come by the same route and settle on the side nearest home (Pons, 1969). Where authority at home is based on seniority, migrants associate with their age-mates and are subject to sanctions imposed by their elders (Mayer, 1971). 'Improvement associations' of townsmen with a common rural background have interested students of Africa for many years, and they have been studied more recently in Latin America. Such organizations keep alive the sense of common identity which implies a respect for the standards of one's peers, as well as having the function that the descriptions more often mention, of providing support for members in trouble and contributing, for example by paying for the education of local boys, to the 'advancement' of the home community; or, as is reported from Peru, to its political defence.

Nevertheless, development advisers with western values find the inhabitants of third world slums deficient in a virtue which they call civic consciousness, as may well be the case in the slums of the rich countries. This is the virtue that creates the array of voluntary associations in an American small town, and that Banfield found to be so deplorably lacking in their counterparts in southern Italy. A project sponsored by the Ford Foundation was launched in Delhi in 1958 with the cooperation of the municipal corporation and its community development staff. Its aims included 'the social integration of the community on a local neighbourhood basis through participation in self-help and mutual aid programs' and 'development of a sense of local pride by stimulating local interest in civic betterment campaigns'. This was to be done by creating a series of councils and by the development of a 'health and welfare council and community chest' (Clinard and Chatterjee, 1961 p. 88). Community chests, we were told, are well known all over the world. I do not think they exist in Britain, where I have never heard one mentioned. They appear to be local welfare funds financed by private contributions.

The Delhi Project workers went from door to door asking people what they considered to be the problems of their neighbourhood and whether they would like to do something about them. It would have been harder to discover in a brief interview what they themselves expected could be achieved by such small money gifts as their informants could spare. The project workers identified local leaders, organized discussion groups and set people going on small-scale improvements. They stimulated 'recreation and handicrafts'–'volley-ball, singing, sewing, weaving and soapmaking'. Help was offered with strings attached; for example, women clubbed together to buy a sewing-machine, and were given a contribution to the cost provided each women agreed to teach two others to sew. 'Since the machines are owned by the group', we are told, 'they are well cared for' (Clinard and Chatterjee, 1961, p. 85). How different from the tractors on collective farms.

This enthusiastic description was published not long after the scheme was launched. In reading it one must bear in mind that government servants have to record successes. One may also reflect that if paternalism is to be adjudged an error, a scheme is no less paternalistic when its aim is to make people independent in ways that they would not themselves have chosen.

If I have laid too much emphasis on some rather absurd frills of the Delhi Project, I should mention that it gave priority to the kind of improvement which slum dwellers are well aware that they need–clearing drains, mending water taps and pumps, levelling and paving streets, repairing houses. It did not and could not attempt to abolish the slum as such, the policy ideal of so many town planners. Every city authority today lays down minimum standards of materials to be used, space allowed per person, and so on, and shanty towns of course fall short of these. A British architect, however (Turner, 1970), recently startled the United Nations by arguing, in the context of the squatter settlements (*barrios*) of Latin America, that to insist on such standards in the economic circumstances of the LDCs might do more to aggravate their housing problems than to alleviate them. These standards are held to be 'good for' people. Their houses should be weather-proof, not fall down (though some of the most modern have been known to do so), be easy to keep clean and equipped at least with running water and electricity. But it is also assumed that these specifications are what everyone *wants*; and whether this is what they actually want depends on what they are accustomed to see around them and demand for themselves. In the affluent North these requirements are basic essentials, whereas space is a low priority. What people want of a house is 'a hygienic and comfortable shelter'; a couple expect to move once or more from a smaller one to a larger as their children grow. They take for granted the possibility of moving to another city.

These are not the *desiderata*, nor the expectations, Turner observes, of squatter populations, and his observations are not confined to Latin America. Squatters would rather have a large incomplete house than a small complete one; what they want most of all is the property that is their only security where there is no effective social assistance. Here it is important to note that we are dealing with people who have no secure base outside the city, as do Africans, and to some extent Indians, who have rights in the rural areas and expect eventually to return there (even if they never actually do so). Most squatters do not expect to move as their family numbers increase; the settlement, and their claim in it, is their sole guarantee of any kind of permanence. They do not pay rent, and they do not live in fear of eviction (unless the whole area is 'slum-cleared', as does not seem to be contemplated for the *barrios* at present). The resources which they would have expended on rent can be put into the gradual completion of their homes. In contrast, municipal authorities must charge rent to recover at least some of the cost of building to approved standards, so that, although better housed, their tenants may be as insecure as they were in the slum; and further, they cannot afford the resources to house all the newcomers, so that a couple applying for a 'council house' may have to wait their turn until their children are grown up.

Turner, then, advocates what he calls 'progressive' housebuilding by individual initiative, beginning as early as possible in the life of a family, in preference to the 'instant' provision of complete housing built to an externally imposed standard. The policy that he favours would be for municipal authorities to accept the existence of these spontaneously created settlements and take responsibility for their administration, as has already been done in many cases in Latin America; in Peru they are designated *pueblos jovenes*, 'young towns'. This has not solved all problems; community decisions in the *barrios* may still be overruled by higher authority, and radical critics say, as they have said of 'community develop-

ment' elsewhere in the world, that to encourage 'self-help' is
just another way of making the poor pay for what should come
to them from the taxes of the rich. But we can at least learn
from these 'do-it-yourself' communities how the people whom
it is proposed to help actually perceive their own needs.

Slums of Hope

A 'theory of slums' propounded in 1962 (Stokes, cited Lloyd,
1979) divides them into 'slums of hope' and 'slums of despair'.
In the latter. one would find the dropouts from society,
displaying the apathy characteristic of the so-called 'culture of
poverty'; their population is downwardly mobile. In the former
are the upwardly mobile, at least in intention and expectation;
they have come to the city for self-improvement, and by
establishing themselves with some source of livelihood–not
necessarily wage labour–have demonstrated some capacity for
achievement. Lloyd has called his study of shanty towns *Slums
of Hope?*. His question-mark implies that we do not know
nearly enough about the actual hopes of the new urban
populations. What frustrations do they experience? Are there
aspects of their present situation that they do not wish
authority to change? Should efforts to improve their lot take
different directions?

The slums of despair are typically those of the central areas
of cities, those which have been left in their original condition,
or worse, cleared by bulldozers in order to beautify the city, or
turn land values to better account, or even, perhaps, with a
conception of the welfare of their inhabitants in mind. The
shanty towns on the edge of the city are the escape from the
squalor and insecurity of dependence on slum landlords that
those slum-dwellers who have not lost hope have found for
themselves. They have grown up in areas where there was
vacant land to build on for three reasons: because such housing
as was offered had been built to a standard that made the rent
impossibly high, because people had to wait too long for
government housing, and because such housing provided
amenities that the well-to-do considered essential, but not
those that the new migrants wanted. Although photographs of

them would horrify any western or UN housing expert, they are valued as homes by the people who live in them.

In the last few years much attention has been given to the 'squatter settlements' (*barrios*) on the fringes of Latin American cities. These are indeed a remarkable phenomenon, since they have not grown up haphazard, but have been created by the concerted action of those inhabitants of inner city slums who did not despair but found their way out, with the tacit consent of the authorities. Mangin (1970) gives an account, based on the experiences of one of his informants, of the formation of a typical *barrio* in Lima. This man, whom he calls Blas, was on the point of losing his rented house because the landlord intended to pull it down and build a cinema. Blas joined a group to which one of his workmates belonged, who were collecting fifty families to 'invade' a vacant area (the term 'invasion' is now recognised as a technical one). They duly did so, on the night before a three-day public holiday which would give them time to settle in. The police ordered them to move but did not force them to; by that time (1954) the Peruvian government had decided to tolerate this solution to the problem of overcrowding. At the end of the three days most of them had set up their straw houses, and some had built brick walls round their plots. The leaders of the movement, about 15 men, had decided in advance where the streets should go and how the plots should be allotted, and when the invaders arrived they marked out the lines of the streets. A committee was elected to speak for the squatters to official authority; this is described as if it had been a spontaneous expression of popular democracy, but in fact official recognition of the *barrio* as a community presupposes the existence of such a committee.

A study made in Venezuela (Ray, 1969) observes that a single leader of the boss type is apt to establish himself as the ultimate authority within a *barrio*. Such a man (called *cacique* like an Indian chief) commonly has the support of the dominant political party in the city, which may even subsidise him, and he maintains his following by his ability to deal with outside authority on their behalf. In return he is able to organise them for self-help activities which would probably not arise from their spontaneous co-operation.

Ray deplores the 'dependent' attitude of people who look to

favours from the *cacique* instead of demanding results in the manner of independent-minded democrats. Here is the same demand for conformity to the western pattern that others make in setting standards of housing. In Italy this kind of dependence is called *clientelismo*. In India it was observed in another form by Bailey (1963), who writes of the 'broker'–the literate, more sophisticated, villager who can help his fellows with applications for the benefits to which they are entitled, and who can deliver to a political party the votes of people indebted to him. This is called 'corruption', and is deplored by the high-minded, and even by the less idealistic if they do not benefit from it. But it oils wheels as well as palms. In those LDCs where bureaucratic institutions are inadequate to provide the development and welfare services for which they have been set up, they would not function without it.

Typical as they are of Latin America, in a world context the *barrios* are exceptional in that they have been created in most cases by a deliberate and organized manoeuvre. Once established they may attract individuals from the countryside, but their founders have been people who first tried the inner city and then either found it intolerable or lost their footing there. Lloyd (1979) suggests that later generations may well see them as a prison rather than a refuge, but at present the slum dwellers are building at their own pace the kind of dwellings that they want to live in. 'Given the right circumstances', says Turner (1970) 'development to "contemporary standards" will take place, even if slowly.' Moreover, the 'invaders' create a community with its own standards and with common interests, at least *vis-à-vis* the urban authorities. This may also be true, however, of inner city slum areas, such as that in central Lagos, the removal of which was observed by Peter Marris (1961, 1974).

Slum Clearance in Singapore

In contrast to the Latin American governments with their *laissez-faire* attitude, Singapore from the moment of independence embarked on a crash housing programme, of which it was said in 1972 that a new flat was put up every 25 minutes.

One new settlement, or rather the re-settlement that it necess-
itated, is described in detail by Gamer (1972). This was in the
Kallang Basin, an area of about a square mile the greater part
of which was under water at high tide. The land was to be
reclaimed from the sea, and an industrial estate developed on
it. Although the project hung fire for some time, when it was
finally adopted it was put through as fast as the reclamation
work could get going.

Above high-water mark lived some three thousand families,
small farmers, fishermen, small businessmen or wage earners in
the city. Areas had been designated in different parts of the
island for the allocation of plots to farmers. One such, a hill
known as Tao Payoh, close to the Kallang Basin, was earlier said
to be 'the most fertile land on the island'. Earth from the top of
this hill was taken to fill in the Basin, and the flat area created
by the bulldozers was covered by a housing scheme.

The Kallang area, although some of its inhabitants were
wage earners, had also the characteristics of a village the
occupants of which found at least part of their livelihood at
home. Some had lived in it a long time. A date was fixed for
them to move; it had to be postponed more than once. By way
of warning, residents were sent forms asking for the numbers in
their families, presumably as a basis for calculating the
numbers to be rehoused and the sum that would be required in
compensation for the removal. They did not reply. Then the
chief architect of the Housing Board recommended that the
trucks with their loads of earth to fill the basin should begin to
move in and thus create the necessary 'psychological effect'.

Finally, notices were distributed announcing that all dwellings in the area would be demolished on a fixed day; and when
the day came, eighty huts were destroyed in the presence of
their owners. 'The land fill operation', wrote Gamer (1972, p.
103, 'was never slowed by the presence of a housing structure.'

Before this, however, settlement officials had visited Kallang
and offered new accommodation in flats. Most of the families
approached did not want to move into flats. A large number
said they would make their own arrangements. Persons
adjudged to be genuine farmers were entitled to plots in rural
resettlement areas, plots of a size which, according to the
statement of a Singapore Livestock Farmers' Association, was

insufficient. Five such offers are on record. There is no record of the numbers who actually took up the accommodation offered by the Housing Board, though there are records of those who refused it because the rents were too high.

These rents were graded according to the number of rooms, the smallest having only one. Slightly larger flats were built later for 'resettlement cases' who 'could not afford higher rents despite their large families' (Gamer, 1972, p. 118). Since at least one-third of the Kallang families numbered six or more, it might be guessed that slum conditions would soon appear in the new housing blocks, seven to fifteen floors high.

Another difficulty with high-rise building arose when small-scale factories were offered floor-space in a seven story building at subsidised rents. In Kallang these enterprises had been carried on in and around the employers' houses. The workmen lived in shacks alongside and the materials were spread out in the open air. It proved impossible to organise the work in a confined space, and it spread out all over the passageways, blocking communication. This experiment was soon given up.

From Cairo comes another account of the inconveniences in the eyes of villagers of living in flats. Like the *barrio* dwellers, they think of a home as a small number of enclosed rooms with an interior courtyard where people cook, eat or sit at leisure. There is a room with an oven where the family sleep in cold weather. In town they are driven into the street for all the activities they have been used to carry on out of doors. Some of them try to get topfloor flats so that they can build an oven on the roof (Abu-Loghud, 1972).

Slum clearance in Africa

The Kallang Basin story illustrates a type of 'urban renewal' which concentrates on the new use to be made of an area and gives little thought to the needs, let alone the wishes, of the people to be removed from it. Two writers on Africa, the sociologist Peter Marris (1961, 1974) and the anthropologist Philip Mayer (1971) have described the effect on slum populations of removal to housing estates built to receive them. In each case, though the move may have been thought to be in the people's interests, the actual operation was prompted by other considerations. It was the imminence of independence celeb-rations that led the Nigerians to think visitors should not be confronted with squalor in the centre of the capital, and it was for the implementation of South Africa's apartheid policy that the labour force of East London in the Cape Province was moved from the doorstep of the city to a 'new town' in the Ciskeian homeland.

The Lagos slum dwellers were not at the mercy of rack-renting landlords who might decide to destroy their homes and build something else in their place. They had no formal organisation, but they were a closely knit community. The land and houses were owned by Africans. A few houses were still the ancestral homes of extended families. In others, rooms were rented out, and members of less fortunate families contrived to find accommodation where they could keep in daily touch. Formal family meetings were regularly held, when help for needy members was arranged and disputes settled. Well-to-do family heads conducted substantial businesses from their houses, even storing there the goods they imported. Women traded from their doorsteps, and there was plenty of custom from casual passers-by. Many sold cooked food to office workers.

> They had long acquired the city-dweller's skill in improving their own use of buildings designed for another purpose . . . By the layout of its dwellings, designed not for a single household but a group of related households; by the intermingling of domestic life and petty trade; by the compactness of the clusters of family networks; by the indifference to the amenity of the cramped and sparsely furnished rooms . . . by the gregariousness of its streets, central Lagos expressed beautifully the values and meanings of the lives it sheltered. (Marris, 1974, pp. 56, 50)

Many of these slum dwellers chose to go to rural areas or smaller towns where they had kin; some tried to resist eviction, and were trounced by the local newspaper: 'By indulging foolhardiness, they had only themselves to blame if the police, with Nigeria behind them, got the better of them' (*Daily Times*,

cited Marris, 1974, p. 56). Those who did go to Surulere, the
new estate, found themselves cut off from the bustle of the city
and from contact with those kin and friends who lived outside
the cleared area. Trading from houses was forbidden, and in
any case there was no custom. Domestic supplies had to be
bought in a single large shopping centre. The substantial
business men could not manage their affairs at a distance; some
went bankrupt. Rents, amenities, and travelling to work cost
more, as they do in all newly built housing estates. The new
amenities were indeed welcomed by those who were dissatisfied
before—young men earning salaries, who could pay for them,
and who were glad to be independent of older kinsmen, lodgers
from other parts of Nigeria who had felt alien in the life of the
common compound. This is a striking example of a project
which caused hardship to the more conservative that may be
regarded as only temporary, since the way of life that they have
lost is passing in any event. It is one of the cases in which the
anthropologist may be accused of an obstructive predilection
for the old-fashioned point of view. He could reply that, since
this is a question of human suffering, its existence ought at least
to be known to those who cause it, whether or not they consider
it to be inevitable. And he would certainly agree with Marris in
condemning the cruelty (his word) of policies which deliberately shake up a community with the idea that to do so will
forcibly modernize them; short, sharp shocks never created a
new type of human being. Those who use the phrase perhaps
forget that it was coined by W. S. Gilbert, a man of no fine
sensibility, to describe execution by beheading.

   Mayer's account of the clearance of the East London shanty-
town mentions some similar consequences. In particular the
distance from work of the 'new town' Mdantsane was even
greater because of the requirements of apartheid, and the
transport facilities even worse. Here those most disorganized
were the so-called Reds—not Communists but red-blanketed
Xhosa who had lived in the most dilapidated part of the
location, resisting assimilation to town ways, which they
considered immoral, by forming small close groups to drink
together after work and 'talk about home'. The members of
these groups now lived far apart; they were afraid to go out at
night for fear of being mugged by the young hooligan '*tsotsis*';

and in any case they usually got home too late for much sociability. Here again, Mayer points out that many circumstances combine to make the Red way of life unattractive to the younger generation. One of the advantages of Mdantsane was the provision of schooling, which had not yet come to be resented on account of the imposition of the Afrikaans language. It was becoming harder and harder to make a living from farming, and in a period when the South African economy was booming there were good prospects for literate Africans. Mayer foresaw that the 'Red' attitude, deliberately rejecting literacy and all that goes with it, would disappear before long; it may have already done so, though the latest news of the new 'homeland' township no longer describes a booming economy. But the tendency of 'home-boys' to congregate together when they are in employment far from home has not disappeared and will not. This is a source of the cohesion of small groups through which social order is maintained through informal pressures. To try to use the removal of a population as a means to break down this cohesion in the interests of a wider one is a recipe for *anomie*. One or two sociologists have suggested that slum-cleared populations might be moved as *groups* and allowed to choose their neighbours in their new surroundings. This might or might not be practicable. But more dialogue with beneficiaries who so often prove to be victims, and more knowledge of their circumstances, would indubitably be practicable and would never be wasted.

Gamer's discussion of the Kallang Basin Project refers to unasked and unanswered questions (1972, p. 127). His book is possibly unique in offering the reader a page (65) of questions that might have been asked. Here are some of them:

What was life like for the people in the Basin [a rather wide question perhaps]?
Where they extorted [sic] by criminal elements?
Was there reason to believe that there would be less (or more?) extortion as a result of the reclamation project?
How did they get along with their neighbours?
Was there reason to believe that they would get along better (or as well?) as a result of the reclamation project? . . .

Did the young people in the Basin study their homework?
Was there reason to believe that they would study as much after the reclamation project?
What were living conditions like in their houses?
Would their living conditions be better as a result of their moving?

These are second-order questions. More basic data on social structure would have to be gathered before they could be answered, such as the nature of existing solidary groups; and more basic economic data, though Gamer does give us some information there.

A conclusion that might be drawn from these observations on slums and how to deal with them is that, if it is possible to improve the conditions in which people are living as a community, this is greatly preferable to decanting them into new surroundings; particularly if, as happens more often than not, the community is disrupted by the move. Sometimes the decanted populations have simply seeped back again.

It may not always be possible to reclaim the slums of inner cities; even the affluent world is not finding it too easy. Where a slum area is cleared because the site could be made to yield a greater return, it is a matter of ethical values, not of specialist knowledge, to judge between such a policy and one that would have more regard for the people whose lives will be immediately affected. Anthropologists, since they have lived in contact with such people and observed their reactions, are inclined to place their interests first. But this does *not* mean that they say, as they have so often been supposed to say, 'the natives are always right'. In countries where authority does not tell us what we must think, we all have to decide for ourselves who is right, but it is as well that we should decide with as much knowledge as possible, and an important part of that knowledge can be provided by anthropologists.

10
Envoi

This book has been written with the implied qualification 'other things being equal'; that is to say, it assumes an environment in which the makers of policy sincerely wish *both* to increase general productivity *and*, as far as they can, to better the lot of the poorest among their people. Even more important, it assumes an environment in which this will be possible. It assumes that laws will be made, not for show, but with the intention of enforcing them. It assumes a sufficient degree of security of life and limb for poor farmers to find it worth their while to make the improvements that are recommended to them; perhaps this actually exists more widely than news reports, necessarily concentrating on what disturbs everyday life, lead us to imagine. It assumes a certain level of competence among bureaucrats which may actually be lacking, at any rate in some of the smaller third world countries; and a certain level of probity among foreign bringers of 'help'. It assumes a willingness to tackle the many problems which ready made solutions have not solved. Who can tell how far, or where, in the third world, these conditions are fulfilled? I have written this book for those who hope, or wish, to see that they are.

Bibliography

Abu-Loghud, J. (1972) 'Migrant Adjustment to City Life', in G. Breese (ed.), *The City in Newly Developing Countries* (London: Prentice-Hall).

All-India Rural Credit Survey (1954) *Report of the Committee of Direction*, vol. II (Bombay).

Apthorpe, R. (1969) 'Peasants and Planistrators in Eastern Africa', *Bulletin of the Institute of Development Studies*, vol. 1, no. 3.

Azad, R. N. (1978) *Objectives and Strategies for Rural Development and Agrarian Reform with Special Emphasis on Participation of the Rural Poor*, Expert Group Meeting on Agrarian Reform and Rural Development (Bangkok: FAO).

Bailey, F. G. (1957) *Caste and the Economic Frontier* (Manchester University Press).

Bailey, F. G. (1963) *Politics and Social Change* (Oxford University Press).

Barker, R. (1978) 'Barriers to Efficient Capital Investment in Agriculture', in T. W. Schultz, (ed.), *Distortions in Agricultural Incentives* (Bloomington: Indiana University Press).

Barrett, S. (1979) 'The Politics of Defection from an African Utopia', *Africa* no. 49.

Berreman, G. (1972) *Hindus of the Himalayas* (Berkeley: University of California Press).

Bray, F. A. and Robertson, A. F. (1980) 'Share cropping in Kelantan, Malaysia', *Research in Economic Anthropology*, vol. 3.

Campbell, D. J. (1981) 'Land-Use Competition at the Margins of the Rain Lands', in G. Norcliffe and T. Pinfold, *Planning African Development* (London: Croom Helm).

Carruthers, I. (1976) 'Water Supplies and Irrigation' in J. Heyer (ed.), *Agricultural Development in Kenya* (Nairobi: Kenya Institute for Development Studies).

Chambers, R. (ed), (1970) *The Volta Resettlement Scheme* (London: Pall Mall Press).

Cleave, J. H. (1974) *African Farmers: Labour Use in the Development of Small-Holder Agriculture* (London: Praeger).

Clinard, N. B., and Chatterjee, B. (1961) in R. Turner (ed.), *India's Urban Future* (University of California Press).

Cohen, A. (1969) *Custom and Politics in Urban Africa* (London: Routledge & Kegan Paul).

Colson, E. (1958) *Marriage and the Family among the Plateau Tonga* (Manchester University Press).

Colson, E. M. (1971) *The Social Consequences of Resettlement* Manchester University Press).

Davis, J. (1973) *Land and Family in Pisticci* (London: Athlone Press).

De Kadt, E. (1974) 'Introduction', in E. De Kadt and G. Williams (eds), *Sociology and Development* (London: Tavistock).

De Wilde, J. C. (1967) *Experiences with Agricultural Development in Tropical Africa* (Baltimore: Johns Hopkins University Press).

Elkan, W. (1978) *Development Economics* (Harmondsworth: Penguin).

Emecheta, B. (1977) *The Slave Girl* (London: Allison & Busby).

Epstein, T. S. (1962) *Economic Development and Social Change in South India* (Manchester University Press).

Epstein, T. S. (1973) *South India Yesterday, Today and Tomorrow* (London: Macmillan).

Evans-Pritchard, E. E. (1951) *Kinship and Marriage among the Nuer* (Oxford: The Clarendon Press).

Fortes, M. (1949) *The Web of Kinship among the Tallensi* (Oxford University Press).

Freeman, J. D. (1958) 'The Family System of the Iban of Borneo', in J. Goody (ed), *The Developmental Cycle in Domestic Groups* (Cambridge University Press).

Fuller, C. (1976) *The Nayars Today* (Cambridge University Press).

Gamer, R. E. (1972) *The Politics of Urban Development in Singapore* (Cornell University Press).

Geertz, C. (1963) *Peddlers and Princes* (Chicago University Press).

Gluckman, M. (1963) *Order and Rebellion in Tribal Africa* (London: Cohen & West).

Harris, B. (1961) 'Centralisation and Planned Development', in R. Turner (ed.), *India's Urban Future* (University of California Press).

Harrison, R. K. (1978) 'Work and Motivation', in D. J. Murray (ed.), *Studies in Nigerian Administration* (London: Hutchinson).

Heady, E. O. (1978) Comment on Barker, in T. W. Schultz (ed.), *Distortions of Agricultural Incentives* (Indiana University Press).

Hill, P. (1969) 'Hidden Trade in Hausaland', *Journal of the Royal Anthropological Institute*, n.s., vol. 4, no. 3.

Hoben, A. (1973) *Land Tenure among the Amhara of Ethiopia* (Chicago University Press).

Hobson, S. (1978) *Family Web* (London: Murray).

Holt, J. and Abdalla, A. J. (1981) 'A Study of the Spontaneous Settlement of Nomads in Western Sudan: Interim Report', mimeo. (London: International African Institute).

HMSO (1975) *Overseas Development: The Changing Emphasis in British Aid Policies: More Help for the Poorest*, Cmnd 627 (London).

Hunter, G. (1970) *The Administration of Agricultural Development* (Oxford University Press).

Indian Council of Social Science Research (1978) *Role of Rural Women in Development* (Delhi: Allied Publishers).

Jasny, N. (1949) *The Socialised Articulture of the USSR* (Stanford University Press).

Jay, R. (1969) *Javanese Villagers: Social Relations in Rural Madjokuto* (Cambridge, Mass: MIT Press).

Jiggins, J. (1977) 'Motivation and Performance of Extension Field Staff', in *Extension, Planning, and the Poor* (Overseas Development Institute, Agricultural Administrative Unit, Occasional Paper 2).

Johnson, A. W. (1971) *Sharecroppers of the Sertao* (Stanford University Press).

Kolakowski, L. (1978) *Main Currents of Marxism* (Oxford: Clarendon Press).

Le Vine, B. A. (1966) *Dreams and Deeds* (Chicago University Press).

Lipton, M. (1974) 'Towards a Theory of Land Reform', in Lehmann (ed.), *Agrarian Reform and Agrarian Reformism* (London: Faber).

Lipton, M. (1977) *Why Poor People Stay Poor* (London: Temple Smith).

Lloyd, P. C. (1974) *Power and Independence* (London: Routledge & Kegan Paul).

Lloyd, P. C. (1979) *Slums of Hope? Shanty Towns in the Third World* (Harmondsworth: Penguin).

Long, N. (1968) *Social Change and the Individual* (Manchester University Press).

Long, N. (1977) *An Introduction to the Sociology of Rural Development* (London: Tavistock).

Lugard, F. D. (1922) *The Dual Mandate in British Tropical Africa* (Edinburgh: Blackwood).

Mangin, W. (1970) 'Urbanisation: a Case History in Peru', in W. Mangin (ed.), *Peasants in Cities* (Boston: Houghton Mifflin).

Marnham, P. (1979) *Nomads of the Sahel* (London: Minority Rights Group).

Marris, P. (1961) *Family and Social Change in an African City* (London: Routledge & Kegan Paul).

Marris, P. and Somerset, A. (1971) *African Businessmen* (London: Routledge & Kegan Paul).

Marris, P. (1974) *Loss and Change* (London: Routledge & Kegan Paul).

Mayer, P. (1971) *Townsmen or Tribesmen*, 2nd edn (Oxford University Press).

Minogue, K. (1980) 'The Rhetoric of Goodwill', *Encounter*, December 1980.

Nadel, S. F. (1942) *A Black Byzantium* (Oxford University Press).

Nelson, M. (1973) *The Development of Tropical Lands: Policy Issues in Latin America* (Baltimore: Johns Hopkins University Press).

Nyerere, J. (1962) *Ujama'a: The Basis of African Socialism*, reproduced in W. H. Friendland and C. G. Rosberg (1964) *African Socialism* (Stanford University Press).

Pauw, B. A. (1963) *The Second Generation* (Cape Town: Oxford University Press).

Peel, J. D. Y. (1980) 'Inequality and Action: The Forms of Ijesha Social Control', *Canadian Journal of African Studies*, no. 14.

Pocock, D. (1972) *Kanbi and Patidar* (Oxford: Clarendon Press).

Pons, V. (1969) *Stanleyville* (Oxford University Press).

Ray, T. F. (1969) *The Politics of the Barrios of Venezuela* (University of California Press).

Rimmer, D. (1981) '"Basic Needs" and the Origins of the Development Ethos', *Journal of Developing Areas*, no. 15. The phrase quoted is his comment in discussion of this article.

Schuh, G. E. (1978) 'Alternative Approaches to Equity', in T. W. Schultz (ed.), *Distortions of Agricultural Incentives* (Indiana University Press).

Schumacher, E. F. (1973) *Small is Beautiful* (London: Blond & Briggs).

Scudder, T. (1962) *The Ecology of the Gwembe Tonga* (Manchester University Press).

Scudder, T. (1975) 'Resettlement', in N. F. Stanley and M. P. Alpers (eds), *Man-Made Lakes and Human Health* (London: Academic Press).

Scudder, T. (1980) 'Policy Implications of Compulsory Relocation in River Basin Development Projects' in M. Cernea and P. B. Hammond (eds), *Projects for Rural Development: The Human Dimension* (Baltimore: Johns Hopkins University Press, for World Bank).

Seers, D. (1969) *The Meaning of Development* (University of Sussex: Institute of Development Studies, Communication Series no. 44).

Shue, V. (1980) *Peasant China in Transition* (University of California Press).

Smith, R. T. (1956) *The Negro Family in British Guiana* (London: Routledge & Kegan Paul).

Srinivasan, T. N. and Bardhan, R. K. (1974) *Poverty and Income Distribution in India* (Calcutta: Statistical Publishing Society).

Stavenhagen, R. (ed.) (1970) *Agrarian Problems and Peasant Movements in Latin America* (New York: Doubleday).

Steenland, K. (1977) *Agrarian Reform under Allende* (Albuquerque: University of New Mexico).

Swift, J. (1978) 'The Role of Seasonality in a West African Pastoral Economy', mimeo (University of Sussex: Institute of Development Studies).

Turner, J. (1970) 'Barriers and Channels for Housing Development in Modernizing Countries', in W. Mangin (ed.), *Peasants in Cities* (Boston: Houghton Mifflin).

Turner, V. W. (1967) *The Forest of Symbols* (Cornell University Press).

Van Gennep, A. (French 1908) *The Rites of Passage* (English trans. London: Routledge & Kegan Paul 1960).

Vatuk, S. (1972) *Kinship and Urbanization* (University of California Press).

Weinrich, A. K. H. (1975) *African Farmers in Rhodesia* (Oxford University Press).

Werbner, R. B. (1970) 'Land and Chiefship in the Tati Concession', *Botswana Notes and Records*, vol. 2.

White, G. F., Bradley, D. J., and White, A. U. (1972) *Drawers of Water* (Chicago University Press).

Williams, G. (1974) 'Political Consciousness among the Ibadan Poor', in E. de Kadt and G. Williams (eds), *Sociology and Development* (London: Tavistock).

World Bank (1978) *World Development Report 1978*.

Index